MW00800680

Three
Little
Decisions

Three
Little
Decisions

How to Move Beyond the Bruises of Life

JANET K. MARKS

credo
house publishers

Three Little Decisions
Copyright © 2018 by Janet K. Marks
All rights reserved.

Published in the United States by Credo House Publishers,
a division of Credo Communications, LLC, Grand Rapids, Michigan
credohousepublishers.com

Scripture is taken from the HOLY BIBLE, NEW INTERNATIONAL
VERSION®. NIV®. Copyright © 1973, 1978, 1984 by International Bible
Society. Used by permission of Zondervan. All rights reserved.

The Merriman Webster Dictionary was used for dictionary definitions.

While all stories in this book are true, most names and identifying
information have been changed to protect the privacy of the individual.

ISBN: 978-1-625860-90-3

Cover and interior design by Frank Gutbrod
Editing by Elizabeth Banks and Cecile Higgins
Interior pear illustration by Stephanie K. Marks
Cover image by Clem Onojeghuo/Unsplash.com

Printed in the United States of America
First edition

When I was twenty, there was a young man who said he believed one day I'd write a book. I scoffed in disbelief and told him, "No way! I could never do that."

Undeterred, he said he imagined God would use me to teach and speak before scores of people. To that I cringed and countered, "Never! I wouldn't know what to say."

Life lesson learned: Never—say—never! Obviously that man's faith in God was great. That man went on to walk beside me in life as my adored husband.

All he believed and dreamed for me has become true. To Tom, my dreamer, my love and lifelong best friend, I am honored God allows me to traverse through life with you.

Here's the book, Babe.

Contents

Introduction — Gales of Change

Every day, do something that will inch
you closer to a better tomorrow.

— Dr. Doug Firebaugh

Life is a series of decisions made every day, whether they are conscious or not—little choices we rarely consider—until something shakes us out of our tedium. Some decisions are forced upon us, they are unwelcome and demand change. Like pulling back a heavy quilt on a cold winter morning, the chill of change shocks our system and jolts us awake. It forces us to face a new reality and moves us into unfamiliar territory. We feel unsure how to proceed; we shiver and scratch our head, wondering what just happened to our world.

Several years ago, an unexpected change came into my life. This change did not arrive as a gentle knock on my front door, but instead kicked it down and roared in like an arctic blast, freezing me to the bone. It was a bleak January morning when my husband, Tom, and I were unexpectedly dismissed from our jobs as Christian ministry leaders. To some, this may seem like an inconsequential change, but those fateful words, "We're going another direction," ended three decades of service, dedication, and our life's work.

I was stupefied. A thick fog of incomprehension gathered as I attempted to digest this news. On the drive home, I saw only the gray haze of that January morning. As the fog began to lift, I realized we had, in one fell swoop, lost both incomes and what we thought would be a lifelong career. Like the puff of smoke after a candle is snuffed—visible one moment and then gone in a single breath. The acrid smell of the smoke tightened around my heart.

I was in new territory and it terrified me. Every thought now circled around the question: *What had I done wrong?* What would the change mean for my children, my relationships with fellow believers . . . or my relationship with God? Unexpectedly, I found I dreaded attending church, which was a new feeling, since I had enjoyed that part of my life as long as I could remember. Despite the dread, we continued to attend church services hoping to remain connected to those we loved, but it only reminded me of the loss and brought on more anguish. And when the church sang hymns filled with beautiful harmonies and words of God's unending love, it dislodged a boulder in my heart and unleashed an avalanche of emotion—I could not turn off the tears. On some Sundays, Tom and I would pull our Honda into the parking lot where the congregation was meeting and just sit in the car, neither of us having the fortitude to go inside. A few times we even chose to drive away.

The Brick Wall

Some call such a wild swing of emotions *reversal*—you're going 100 mph in one direction, hit a metaphorical brick wall, and are knocked senseless. At some point in life, most of us hit a wall like this. For some, it may be the unanticipated duty of caring for an ailing parent or sick child. It might be the death of a loved one, a job loss, a ruined relationship, financial collapse, or a personal health crisis. Whatever the change, any great loss or crisis pitches us against that wall and knocks us sideways. Recovery comes more slowly than ever imagined.

After I hit this wall, something changed inside; it was as if an essential part of my identity had been knocked away, and I was unsure how to proceed. The initial shock was followed by weeks of a frantic pursuit of other career options, which turned into months of dissecting the reasons for having to do so. It included murky periods of hiding from, avoiding, and occasionally mudslinging at those who had wounded me. When we're in this kind of pain, it's so easy to justify our sour reactions as *acceptable* or at least *allowable*. And if we aren't vigilant, these injuries fester into a full-blown pit of resentment, which is right where I landed. Bitterness took root; and as happens with bitterness, I pushed people away and misery reigned.

Genuine friends pressed in, despite my sour state of mind. They urged me to move on and away from the bitterness. But how could I do this? I felt trapped in a vicious riptide, pulling me fast and far from the person God wanted me to be. Fear gripped my heart as it grew clear how far out to sea I'd drifted; I begged God not to let me drift so far that I might never find my way back to him. My friends continued to pour out their love and kindness, and they reminded me to keep my eyes on God's plan for my life. Exhausted from the battle, I strained to see his beacon of light and prayed for strength to once again find his harbor of peace.

A Tiny Miracle

As God is so inclined, his answer to my prayers emerged through a back channel. There was no booming voice from heaven but a quiet peep like the sweet yawn of a newborn. Somewhere in those dark days, my friend Maggie gave me a woven basket filled with small wrapped gifts for my birthday. She couldn't have known the impact one of the items would have on me. The gift was a spiral notepad titled, *Three Things to Do Today!* As it instructed, each day I dutifully wrote down three things to do and found unexpected pleasure as I crossed off each completed item. They weren't huge, life-altering decisions but small things: make a phone call to someone who makes me laugh, sweep the kitchen floor, or go for a walk. If a task wasn't accomplished, I merely moved it forward to another day. This simple action and repetition helped move me beyond my slump as I realized my success at *something.* They were little things, really. But each small victory gave me a needed boost, and each step helped me stand up straighter and imagine my life having meaning once more.

The tiny miracle arrived as I began to understand there were deeper decisions to consider, substantial decisions I could make that might nudge me closer to a healed soul. *Three things to do* became *three decisions* to make. I knew if I wanted to regain spiritual and emotional health, the destructive habits of bitterness needed to be set aside and positive behaviors solidly put in their place. In my head, I understood God had a plan for my life, but that didn't mean everything was sunshine and bunnies. I struggled along, making my three little decisions even though at times cycles of sadness still coursed through my mind. There were good days when the decisions moved me out of my listlessness and others when my wheels spun with little forward motion. I stood at a crossroads, wondering if I would always stay on this muddled road of confusion or make just *three little decisions* and move forward to new frontiers of hope and faith.

People may say, "What's the big deal? It's just a little decision—how hard can that be?"

Ah, if only it were so simple. Very little about decisiveness is easy, and in flashes of honesty we can admit decision making intimidates us. Sometimes, we worry we'll make a wrong decision so we push it to another day and avoid it altogether! Other times we fear the choice we make will have an undesirable consequence— we hem and haw, wondering if it's the *right* decision. As a result, many choose to simply sidestep any decision making, whether for little decisions or big.

Clarity in decision making is rarely offered as a silver-wrapped gift with a red bow and a tag stating, *Go this way!* We cannot know the outcome of many of the decisions we make; but regardless, we recognize the need to make them. If we keep our eyes and ears (and heart) open, the way to go will be revealed to us; maybe in a whisper from God or in counsel from a trusted friend or perhaps even in a small, spiral notepad. The key is to do *something*, and then something else, taking one step at a time and making one decision at a time.

Three Little Decisions is filled with universal wisdom, which stems from personal stories about real people and is sprinkled with true-to-life humor about our view of life, other people, and ourselves. It draws upon distinctive lessons from which we're able to learn and is designed to prompt small steps, which, prayerfully, will move us *up and off* the proverbial couch.

The Help of Little Decisions

Each chapter closes with an opportunity to make *three little decisions*. These can be any kind of decision: a simple task, a phone call, a small goal, or something more contemplative. Also following each chapter is a section called *Deeper Reflection*, which offers prompts and questions to help lead you toward decisions rich with significance. Any positive decision made is a step in the right direction. Even though it *seems* insignificant, doing a little something nudges you toward the bigger, more meaningful actions and helps you get un-stuck! Remember, doing *something* is more than doing nothing.

My deep hope and earnest prayer is that the lessons I've learned along the way will be of value and encouragement to you on your journey.

A year from now, you will wish you had started today.
—Karen Lamb

Decisions about LIFE

Nobody can go back and start a new beginning.
But anyone can start today and make a new ending.

—Maria Robinson

I t is my strong conviction God wants to show us the good in each day and help us glean the best from every life experience. And who wouldn't want this? I doubt there is anyone who doesn't want to laugh a lot, spend special moments with family and friends, stand in awe of creation, and take simple pleasure in each day. We *want* these things, but at times the challenges of life push in and zap our joy—much like static shock when we walk in socks on new carpet. It makes us hesitant to touch anything or anyone for fear of getting zapped!

But life is full of zaps and zings and full of hard days—days which are not easy to navigate and at times cause us to question how God could call us to *be joyful always!* On such days, we struggle with gratitude, waver in our faith, wrestle with worry, and wonder how we'll ever get through it.

No one likes to be *zapped*! But instead of endlessly hoping for a life with no zaps or challenges, let's take a different tack and find a new outlook. I believe it's all in our approach. For example, when my younger sister Bonny was in high school, she kidded with her friends that she and our dad both drove a *Vette*. The truth was she drove an entry level Chevy *Chevette* while dad drove a *Corvette*. It's all about our point of view.

How do we gain a positive perspective? From my observation, becoming a positive person is a learnable trait—a quality we might attain if we make some effort. For example, if we tell ourselves it's going to be a good day, we are more prone to search for and look for the good. When we find it, our overall outlook becomes brighter and more hopeful, as we realize we are actually having a good day! An optimist deals with the *zaps* in life by constantly looking for the good no matter what they encounter. We won't eliminate all the challenges life throws our way; but as we adjust our response, we will find sweet morsels of good. The choice to adjust is ours.

I am like many people, a glass-half-full kind of person; I typically see the good in a situation and believe the best about others. Sometimes though, when I face certain difficulties, the water in my glass develops a sour taste—suddenly, it's half empty and everything tastes bad. These are the times I must lean on and borrow the faith of others or spend extra time in prayer. Sometimes I get out my journal and write down my troubles, which primes my own deeper reflection. On other days I circle back to elementary truths in Scripture, read about God's love and am reminded of the good he brings to each day. Any of these little decisions help me find my way out of that brown paper bag of negativity.

In section one, *Decisions about Life*, we will address our perspective on those difficult days of negativity, how we might adjust our attitude, and the good we can find in every circumstance.

> *Some people grumble that roses have thorns;*
> *I am grateful that thorns have roses.*
> —Alphonse Karr, author

CHAPTER 1

Habits of Happiness

*Most folks are as happy as they
make up their minds to be.*

—Abraham Lincoln

The Happy Factor

*"Are you happy, Janet?" Oh, how I hated that question, my brows
scowled together as I considered an honest response. I don't know
why it bothered me, but a friend frequently asked me this pointed
question. It was a simple question, loaded with innuendo, and it
sent me into a wild self-analysis of my current happiness level.*

*It was discomfiting, since there were certainly times my happy
factor was low, but I was unable to tell you why. The guilt for not
being happy would pile on because there was no good reason not
to be deliriously happy! I wanted to be happy, should have been
happy, but often, was not.*

*Apparently anyone who has enough money to afford
three meals in a day is wealthier than 97 percent of the world's
population—97 percent! An immigrant from an impoverished
country once told his friend the term "snack" is unheard of in most
of the world. We have so much more than we can fathom! What*

could I possibly be unhappy about? To quote a friend in Dallas, my life is "freakishly" blessed!

A few years ago, I watched a movie about a man—married, talented, and a successful lawyer—who couldn't understand the lack of emotional fulfillment in his life. It befuddled him, because he knew he had been given so much yet felt such discontent. Through a series of events, he discovered a surprising and profound fulfillment through competitive ballroom dancing, but he kept it secret from his wife. As movies go, his wife discovered his new interest. Late one night as they stood in the kitchen of their beautiful suburban home, she questioned, not only why he danced, but also why he had kept it from her. It took him a few moments to answer, but then he spread his arms open to indicate their beautiful home and family. He said to her, "I feel guilty! Guilty for this not being enough."

What is it about this elusive happiness? How similar are we to the man in the movie who longs for more but doesn't understand what *more* is? The lack of satisfaction we experience is at times puzzling and hard to grasp. Could it be that God allows us a certain level of discontentment to remind us this world is not our final stop? Perhaps this longing for fulfillment pushes us deeper, to consider what matters most, and turns our thoughts to God, the One who knows the big picture, the end of the story.

Like waves in the ocean, life has a natural ebb and flow of good times and struggle. How we respond to the ups and downs has a big effect on our personal happiness level. If we are someone who waits for everything to be *good* before we will be content, we're in trouble. Life can never be *all* good. If we believe we'll finally be happy when others treat us the way we want, we'll wait a long time. We cannot make anyone do everything we want, even if we stomp our foot and demand certain treatment. This won't make life better, but instead, will make us a self-absorbed, foot-stomping person whom others try to avoid. Not much happiness here.

It's a funny thing though, when we look out for the needs of others and help meet those needs, it shifts our focus away from us and fills our heart with the warm satisfaction of knowing we've helped someone. Below is a list of ideas we might try:

- Offer a dinner invitation to someone who doesn't have family nearby.
- Fix or buy a meal for someone who is sick or moving.
- Share the bounty from our garden with a neighbor or coworker.
- Buy a bag of groceries for someone having a tough time financially.
- Serve at a food bank or women's shelter.
- Visit someone at a nursing home. Bring a smile to their day.
- Volunteer at an animal shelter.
- Walk across the street and welcome a new family to the neighborhood.
- Donate money to a special cause, or clean out a closet and donate unwanted items.
- Stop and speak to a neighbor.
- Offer to watch the children of a young family, so the parents can enjoy a date night.

When we go out of our way to encourage others, the focus shifts away from our own troubles and gives us a new (and improved) perspective. It nudges us toward gratitude for what we have—even if it's only a small patch of grass by the front door or a soft pillow on which to lay our head at the end of a long day. As we find reasons to be grateful, it turns what we have into *having enough* and helps bring clarity to the confusion.

One culprit attempting to steal all contentment is the qualifier we add to our circumstance. For example, we say, *Sure, I am happy, but* . . . but what? Or the comment, *I like my house, but I wish it had* . . . wish it had what? Or *It's a great job, but if only* . . . if only what? It's an easy hole to fall into, this constant wishing and longing for things to be different. Are we able to be content with what we have, with where we are and who we are *today*? To help erase that gray cloud that shadows every happy thought, we might just decide to end the sentence with no qualifiers. Yes. I'm happy. Period.

Another strike on our contentment is when we seek happiness in the wrong places. If we expect some*one* to make us happy, eventually that person will disappoint and then we will battle anger, regret, or hurt feelings. Or we might think one more pair of shoes will do the trick, only to find, once the newness wears off, all we have left is scuffed shoes and an emptied bank account. Other times, we think if we get the promotion at work, it will force people to respect us and treat us better, only to find they don't. It's simply more responsibility to carry. People and possessions are not happiness makers.

What might raise that happy barometer up a few notches? It may surprise us to discover, being happy starts with a simple *decision* to be cheerful. As we decide to be happy about some element of our life, that one happy thought lifts our heart, brightens our eyes, and allows a peacefulness to flow through our mind. What an approach! . . . to choose gratitude, to choose cheerfulness! We often become happier as we *think* happier thoughts, and that cheerful perspective begins to change us and then impacts the people around us. In the iconic movie, *Mary Poppins*, the Banks children include this quality in their request for a new nanny—"If you want this choice position, have a cheery disposition." Who doesn't want to be around someone like this? It's contagious and uplifting.

It may sound simplistic, but sometimes just the act of smiling helps change our outlook. Go ahead and give it a try—give a big toothy grin. How does it feel? Do it again. Two verses in Proverbs illuminate the importance of the mind in matters of personal happiness:

"A happy heart makes the face cheerful." (Proverbs 15:13)
"A cheerful look brings joy to the heart." (Proverbs 15:30)

It goes both ways! The act of placing a cheerful look on our face helps our heart be happier. And when we choose to carry happiness in our heart, it shows up on our face. It's a win-win situation!

The question begs to be asked, *Are you happy?* Hopefully it can be answered in the affirmative. But to pose it differently, *why not be happy?* Really, why not? Why not choose this path and become a joyful and happy person? It does not have to depend on anything or anyone but ourselves. It is our choice. How can we adjust our happy gauge? Which decisions can be made to incline our mind toward happiness today?

How we respond to life's ups and downs has a big impact on our personal happiness.

Three Little Decisions

1.

2.

3.

For Deeper Reflection

When you find yourself constantly longing for circumstances to be different, it's easy to use qualifiers, like, *if only* and *yes, but . . .* Which of these are you able to remove from your vocabulary? You can be content. Even if you are not entirely pleased with your current circumstance, are you able to accept it, find something good in it, and make today better?

Decide to be cheerful and watch it affect your overall demeanor.

CHAPTER 2

Calm in the Crazy

*There are some things you learn best in calm,
and some in storm.*

—Willa Cather

Little Puddles

*More than likely it was postpartum blues. But added to the challenges
of having a newborn, we had just moved to Germany to begin a
mission work, we didn't yet speak the language, we had to find a
school for our five-year-old, and I was unsure where to buy groceries.
The signs posted in the shops were indecipherable and I was unable
to understand the overhead announcements on the subway. Several
times, I lost my way, boarding the wrong train with both kids in the
stroller and ended up on the wrong side of town, tired and worn.
Anxiety remained my constant companion.*

*Clouds of unease scudded through my thoughts as even the
smallest tasks overwhelmed. For instance, when I did finally figure
out where to buy groceries, I worried I would misread a label and
buy cat food instead of canned tuna for sandwiches. Or the time I
took the baby to the doctor and upon leaving the office was unclear of
the diagnosis or the treatment plan. Or the time I attempted to order*

some lunchmeat at the deli but instead ordered three hogs worth! *(Ah, the Metric System—I mean, only an American foreigner would so easily get grams and kilos confused!)*

It's hard to describe the persistent sense of apprehension I felt, but it drove me into a frenzied state of what anyone would describe as an emotional mess. I cried at the drop of a hat; it took just the tiniest provocation to open the faucet in my head and for the tears to spill down my face. Because I cried so easily, one dear friend affectionately called me pfuetzchen, *a German word meaning little puddle (loosely pronounced, pfoots-chen).*

One day I shared my long list of woes with some friends. In their attempt to help me get a grip on my emotions, one of them likened me to a pot of water simmering on a stove—about to boil. Every time the heat increased, the water bubbled over the side of the pot and puddled on the stove. They understood I was facing many new challenges, but they also knew it was vital to find a better way to cope—I would have to find some way to turn down the heat!

Visuals like this are helpful, but my face reddened as my emotional state was described as a pot of water bubbling on a stovetop. Together, we discussed creative ways to turn down the overall temperature of my life. It seemed insurmountable, but I knew I needed to take the first step to calm down!

Culture shock is real, challenging and can bring about a sense of disorientation that takes time and deliberate focus to adjust. I was on information overload with a minimal skill set to respond. When Tom and I reflect on our early years in Germany, we laugh and call it our near-death experience, since we didn't imagine how we'd survive! But despite the challenges we faced, we did survive, and the privilege of living there for several years taught us many valuable life lessons and expanded our understanding of this big world in which we live.

Turning down the temperature is easy to talk about but not as easy to accomplish. There are times when we're thrust into a difficult situation and are bombarded with so much new information we think our mind might burst at the seams. It could be a new job, new relationship, becoming a new mother, or in my case moving to a foreign country. We cannot anticipate every zig or zag of life, but how helpful it is when we're able to find positive and productive ways to manage the overload.

A general definition of stress is a set of negative feelings which, when they accompany a challenging situation, may result in an array of emotional responses. When we accept negative stressors as a *normal* part of our days, it may help us respond better and not be quite as derailed by them. We might also lessen our stress as we practice better time management, find balance between personal and work life, and discover activities which relieve or reduce the pressure.

Society has us believing it's imperative to run every day at full tilt and sprint from one event to the next. We're expected to stay connected and multitask throughout the day. Our reaction to overfilled schedules may include increased levels of anger, frustration, and exhaustion. Some who run too fast in their day-to-day life become pushy and bossy while others find themselves weepy or edgy, as they struggle to keep their emotions at an even keel.

What if, when our pot of water on the stove heats to worried and hurried levels, we search for ways to cool the overall temperature? Think about what soothes and calms? What will it take to bring the heat down? Here are a few ideas that may help:

- Leave home a few minutes earlier than needed to get somewhere on time. There will be less stress about being late, less flying through yellow lights, and less honking at everyone in the way.

- Turn off the TV. It's often an unsatisfying activity that adds to the *heat* without improving the flavor, since so many other tasks don't get accomplished and we feel the stress of not getting them done. Instead of landing on the couch, think of the benefits gained from preparing a healthy meal, taking a short walk, or pursuing a hobby.
- Silence the phone. Turn off all gadgets. Enjoy a few hours of being *unplugged*.
- Take a needed break from reality and read a book, watch a funny movie, call an old friend, or listen to soothing music.
- Drink a cup of hot tea or warm cocoa. Let the warmth of the cup seep into us.
- Go for a walk or a jog.
- Sit and watch as the sun fully sets.
- Go outdoors and look at the night sky. (I love to look at the stars and ruminate about others who have also gazed at them over the centuries.)
- Breathe in deeply, do slow stretches and focus on positive thoughts.
- Dig in the garden, smell the soil, and observe the transformation of the plants.
- Sit and sketch a lovely spot in nature. Whether we are artistic or not, it helps us slow down and think about beauty in creation.
- Write a note to encourage someone who needs a boost.
- I know a woman who loves to clean her home, which helps her to feel all is right in her world. Even if we only declutter a kitchen drawer or tidy the bedroom, it might lighten our mood and calm us.
- Be silent for a few moments and allow God's Spirit to nudge us closer to inner peace and joy. Perhaps we might gracefully remove ourself from a commitment and allow some time for stillness. What if we cleared a morning and had nothing whatsoever on the calendar?

Figure out what works to calm the crazy and then do it. The goal is not to have a stress-free life because there is no one whose life won't boil over from time to time and spill out with emotion. Keep in mind, no one is able to fix all the crazy today, but we are able to *still our hearts* and improve our overall outlook.

Recognize it's within our power to *not* live at a frenetic pace every single day.

Three Little Decisions

1.

2.

3.

For Deeper Reflection

Which friend tells you the *truth* when you need to hear it? Express your gratitude to this friend, let her know your appreciation for her love and watchfulness.

There may be times we fear slowing down because it forces us to think about areas of our life about which we are not proud. Don't let fear stop you from being still. Try to listen to what God's Spirit is telling you.

*I'd like to interject here, *true friends* are people who intentionally listen, don't give pat answers or canned advice, but attempt to help you improve your personal situation. They won't judge but instead provide support and help. Proverb 27:6 says, "Wounds from a friend can be trusted." How grateful we are for friends who tell us the truth about ourselves. I'm glad I have friends who risked my erratic emotions and talked with me about the hot pot of bubbling water.

CHAPTER 3

Transform Fear

I don't run away from a challenge because I am afraid.
Instead, I run toward it because the only way
to escape fear is to trample it beneath your foot.

—Nadia Comaneci

Screaming Down the Mountain

A ski resort in Colorado has added an additional attraction for the tourists after they've spent a day on the slopes: a nighttime snow-tubing slide. It's so steep you can't believe anyone can drop down this vertical shoot and survive! One year, our family joined my sister's family to check it out. As we stood in line, tubes in hand, we laughed nervous giggles. Then as we watched, one by one, the people in front of us dropped out of sight down the mountain. (Did I mention we were required to wear helmets or the fact that we had to sit through a twenty-minute safety presentation? Or that we had to sign a waiver to release the ski resort from all liability, thus adding to the suspense and level of sheer terror?)

As we moved toward the front of the line and peered over the edge, my belly clenched. I wondered how to graciously back out without losing the cool-aunt status with my nieces who smiled up at me; I swallowed hard and sat down on the tube. The guy manning the show grinned and said, "Hang on tight, Lady!" Suddenly I was free-falling down the mountain, the snow-packed walls on either side of the chute kept me on course as I plummeted toward the bottom. I don't remember screaming, but am sure I made numerous promises to God, if only he'd get me through this ride in one piece. Within moments I reached the bottom of the run and glided up the incline to a stop, both exhilarated and surprised at the thrill. After we all reached the exit, we laughed and squealed so hard our faces hurt. It didn't take many moments for us to head back up the hill to do it again! Best vacation ever!

Life can be like this. Some of our experiences exhilarate and so amaze us that we stand in awe or weep with joy. Others wrench our guts and we drop to our knees in despair and wonder how we'll survive. And like the tube run, some do both. No matter which *ride* we've been given, let's decide what will be our best response to those circumstances. Will we overcome our fear, jump in with gusto, and fly down the mountain, or will we hold back and let fear rob us of what could be? Of course, life is never as simple as a tube run, but the similarities are there: the risk, the fear, the thrill, and the *going over the edge.*

As we age we don't stop being afraid, but we fear different things. It's a good practice for each of us to stop and consider *what it is* we fear. As I stood above the tube run, I feared severe bodily harm! That was obvious. But some fears are not so easy to pinpoint, and are at times vague or hard to discern. If someone has emotionally wounded us, we may be afraid to show love or freely give our heart again. If we've been unfairly criticized, we may fear peoples' opinions of us or what they tell others. We fret about our children and our parents. Or perhaps we fear failure and let it hold us back from taking important steps. The truth is clear: everyone has fears of some kind, and if we are able to identify ours, then we greatly increase our chance to conquer those uncertainties and terrors.

Well-of-Worry

How many days do we spend wallowing in the well-of-worry and *what-ifs*? What if we try and fail? What if people think less of us for what we did? What if . . . ? How easy it is to inhabit this dark well and allow entire seasons to pass, as we languish about the what-mights and what-ifs. Once when I was in one of those fearful phases and could only see the dank walls of trouble and the *possible* plight that *might* occur, a friend remarked how much time we waste when we agonize about things no one can control. He suggested I let go of the consuming fear, turn the page, and move on to the next chapter of life. When we do so, not only do we discover what will *actually* happen, but we also take a shot at rewriting the ending.

What a great nugget of truth this was. Turn the page! It was just what I needed to scrutinize the situation and readjust my viewpoint. To climb out of that well-of-worry means we make small decisions every day to identify our fears and then modify our reactions accordingly. As we shine a light into those dark corners, the fears begin to abate—we find they are not nearly as menacing.

Of course, we don't always win the battle over our fears or make the right choices, but we keep at it until our habits change and the fears have less power. Isn't it when we fall and *get back up* that we learn such valuable life lessons? Even when we take small uncertain steps, one after the other, they eventually move us the way we need to go.

People who accomplish significant feats, despite fear or difficulty, are an inspiration. They think long and hard about what it will take to reach their goals. Consider those who train for months to run a marathon or have gone back to school to finish a degree, though it takes years to complete. They need determination and tenacity to not give up when the fear of failure presses in.

I know a woman who struggles every day with chronic pain, yet she still gets up to care for her young family. There's also a woman who lived on the street for a time. She is now employed and collects coats and blankets at her job to deliver to the homeless. Or the snowboarder, who as a teenager contracted meningitis and through the ordeal lost both legs. She didn't let this stop her, but she persevered in her rehabilitation and went on to medal in the Paralympics. What a great story of resolution and perseverance. Another dear woman survived a decade-long, drawn-out divorce battle that included lawsuits and lost custody of her young children. She spent hours in prayer and soul-searching that she might forgive her former husband. Because she's taken the mindset of forgiveness and kindness, she is able to live a joy-filled life with her new husband, has healthy relationships with her grown children, and delights in time spent with her grandkids. It doesn't mean she succeeds every day in the forgiveness arena, but her determination is relentless.

These are people like us. People who seek to overcome their everyday fears and worries and, despite unbelievable obstacles, succeed! Even though success may not come easy, as we adjust our thinking and take steps, even small ones, we'll watch our courage grow! Years ago, as a family, we memorized Joshua 1:9. To this day we quote it with each other whenever we face a new or scary situation, such as starting anything new or a difficulty in a relationship. It helps us remember God is with us, whatever lies ahead.

Have I not commanded you? Be strong and courageous.
Do not be terrified; do not be discouraged,
for the Lord your God will be with you wherever you go.

Today is a good day for courage. Rather than hesitating in fear at the top of the tube-run and wondering if we should push off or not, imagine the sheer delight as we fly past our apprehension and realize all we can accomplish when we step forward!

Take small steps and watch courage grow!

Three Little Decisions

1.

2.

3.

For Deeper Reflection

Pinpoint a concern that lands you in a well-of-worry. What could you do today to modify your thoughts and climb out of that well?

Consider which relationships, situations, or actions make you fearful or cause you to hesitate. How are they keeping you from accomplishing what you want in life?

Think of someone you know who has overcome a great obstacle? What did they do to persevere? What is it about their life that inspires you?

CHAPTER 4

The Downside of Procrastination

*Pile up too many tomorrows, and you'll find
you've collected nothing but a bunch of empty yesterdays.*

—Meredith Wilson

Best Time to Plant a Tree

A speaker asked his audience, "When, do you think, is the best time to plant a tree?"

Various answers rang out. "In the fall!" "In the morning!" "Before the first frost!" And from the joker in the crowd, "When I feel like it!"

It made us all laugh until we realized the speaker was serious and had a somber point to make. As we quieted, he continued, "Really folks—do you know the best time to plant a tree?"

We waited; the expression on his face sobered us. "An ancient Chinese proverb tells us the best time to plant a tree is twenty years ago! But since you can't go back and plant one, then do it today."

His point: do what matters today or at least, take that first step.

Procrastination. It's not the biggest word in the dictionary but it certainly results in big-time consequences. One definition of procrastination is: *the voluntary delay of some important task we intend to do, despite knowing we'll suffer as a result of the delay.* It is self-deception when we wait to do a task and think it will be easier or more convenient later. Will it really get easier to wash the mountain of laundry after several more days? No! We've only added more clothes. Will it ever be easier to start an exercise regimen? No way. We'll be just as tired or sore or busy tomorrow. Tomorrow never comes! And don't think having that difficult conversation with a parent about end-of-life decisions will get any easier. It will not. When we avoid acting on some needed thing, the inaction eventually catches up with us and when it does, the *thing* has grown bigger and more unwieldy.

How will we ever get a task completed if we wait to start next week or until after the holidays? How often do we suppress difficult matters simply because they are distasteful or uncomfortable? Or do we put off doing something important because it feels too big? Writing an overdue letter, reaching out after an argument, eating healthier, taking a class to progress our career, or perhaps even getting out into the yard and planting a tree . . . It's easy to believe we're too tired, too busy, or too broken to accomplish very much. As a result, projects pile up, as does frustration when those tasks go unfinished. What might we accomplish if we stopped waiting and just did *it* today. Could we take one step in that direction?

Logjam

The more we wait, the more those tasks pile up and overwhelm! It's like a logjam in a creek, with broken branches, leaves, and trash caught and unable to move any further. The initial cause for the logjam is not always apparent, generally it's found deep below the water's surface, but the result is easy to see. The debris must be removed one piece at a time to allow the water to freely flow.

This is not dissimilar to a *life* logjam. When we see areas that are backing up and worsening, even when we are unsure what caused the clog, we have some choices to make. It seems easy to ignore the inclination to dig under the surface and address some area that is blocking our personal growth. Or we think we'll deal with the issue later. The problem is, if we continue to sidestep and procrastinate important decisions, eventually that proverbial rain check catches up to us and slows the flow of our joy and fulfilment. This quote by Bobby Maximus is good to consider: *There are seven days in the week. Someday isn't one of them.* When we address the smaller issues, eventually bigger things will become resolved and the current will flow again!

Consider my dear mother, who at the time of this writing is 88 years old. She golfs twice a week (Colorado weather permitting), works out at a gym for women, and rides her stationary bike three to five miles every day. Last year at her gym, they began a competition to see who could hold a *plank* the longest. (This is not a piece of wood, but mom on her forearms and toes, body parallel with the floor, and holding.) Yes, it was mom who won the competition and outlasted everyone, even the much younger owner. At last count, Mom's record was 4.5 minutes. Go ahead, get down on the floor and try this. I last about a minute, nowhere near her record.

Mom didn't start all of this when she was 80. Nor at 70, 60, or 50, but she has been dedicated to her physical fitness throughout her whole life. In the 1940s she lettered in four sports at her Denver high school! As long as I can remember she has been active; she gardened, mowed, did sit ups and leg lifts, and exercised along with the TV program featuring the late Jack LaLanne. It's part of what has made her as strong as she is today. I stand in awe of this woman, and I'm committed to imitating her perseverance and tenacity. The healthy habits develop when we consistently act on the right things. The positive results of these daily decisions are incalculable.

A few years ago, my younger daughter knew I had a tough decision to make about whether or not to leave a difficult job situation. To encourage me, she mailed a fortune from a cookie she'd opened. It said, *Wisdom is knowing what to do next, skill is knowing how to do it, and virtue is doing it.* She knew I needed to act but was holding back due to uncertainty. Her push helped me decide.

Sometimes we need just a little nudge to help move us along.

Three Little Decisions

1.

2.

3.

For Deeper Reflection

In what areas do you procrastinate? Which small action are you able to take today to move forward?

Name one thing that *jams the flow* of your spiritual life. Take a moment to reflect on the reason it is there and why you allow that logjam to remain. What are you willing to do to remove this deterrent and allow the waters of life to flow again?

Trajectory

We are what we repeatedly do.
Excellence, then, is not an act but a habit.

—Aristotle

Choices Made

*For many years I've had the privilege of caring for our elder
population. It's incredible to sit and listen to the indomitable stories
of their lives. These men and women have experienced long lives
filled with family, careers, wars, death, and drought. Some have
responded in amazing ways—being unbelievably pleasant, at peace,
and thankful. My great-aunt Marita, from Wichita, was one of the
sweetest women you would ever meet, and when she developed
Alzheimer's,* she remained so. With a soft Kansas inflection, she
once told a guest in her home, "I don't know you, but I love you."
Oh, to age with such kindness.*

    *Another woman, Deanne, lived in a group home for the
aging and was nearing the end of her life. When it was suggested
she invite her children to come and say their farewells, she became
agitated saying they were good-for-nothings and she'd rather die with*

strangers than have them at her bedside. She was an angry woman. Anyone who did anything to offend her was no longer welcome, and she swore to never speak to them again. We didn't understand the reasons for Deanne's anger nor why she was at odds with her kids. Certainly, her animosity grew over many years, but at some point, the commitment to strengthen the relationships ended, and they all lost out on what might have been.

We know both types of people: those who are pleasant and grateful and those who live out their later years terribly sour. We know which relatives we would rather visit on the holidays. But do we stop to consider how they came to be this way? What clouded the lens through which Deanne looked? What tainted her with disappointment and annoyance? No doubt, we become in our advanced years, the product of how we lived our earlier ones. The results hinge on the choices we've made and those choices directly impact who we become. Will we end up distrustful, resentful, and unwilling to forgive those who have wronged us? Yes, we will, if we are distrustful, resentful, and unwilling to forgive *today*! The good news is the choice to change our actions belongs to us!

It doesn't mean tough days won't sometimes stop us in our tracks or that disappointment will never happen. But it does mean we need to seriously consider *how* we respond to trouble in the here and now. Think of the conversation in *The Christmas Carol*, as Ebenezer Scrooge has a late-night visit by the ghost of his dead business partner, John Marley.

"You are fettered," Scrooge trembled, "Tell me why?"

"I wear the chain I forged in life," replied the ghost. "I made it link by link and yard by yard; I girded it on of my own free will, and of my own free will, I wore it."

Note his words: *I forged, I made, I girded*, and *I wore*. Those were the choices he made, one link at a time. Could such words be said about us? Have we forged a heavy burden, link by link?

The author paints this frightful scene right before three other ghosts take Scrooge on a remarkable journey of redemption. This story is far more than a quaint Christmas tale; we can all benefit from its message by making better choices while we are still able.

Trajectory is a path or line toward a certain point. For this discussion, the *certain point* is where we hope to be in the years ahead. The question becomes, how do we arrive there? Those who are courageous will look closely at how they live right now, and as they do, they will catch a glimpse of who they will become. No, doubt, all of us hope to be full of gratitude, joy, and very little regret. We know what we want to be like, but what we *want* and what we *get* may not end up being the same.

As we consider the decisions made each day, whether significant or not, each decision places us on a course for our life. Wrong choices will take us off course and further away from our goals, costing more than we could imagine.

Contemplate the following diagram of trajectory:

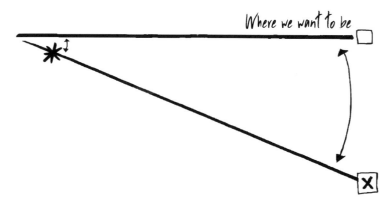

If the star represents where we stand right now and we are only slightly off track, it doesn't seem like a big deal to get back on the best trajectory. It takes less effort to go this short distance. But if we don't adjust and continue the same downward trajectory, we will eventually end up far from where we intended. The X represents where we *may* end up if we don't make the needed modifications. The longer we move away from our goal, the greater effort it takes to claw our way back.

Jesus likened his followers to sheep, which are not known to be incredibly bright, need constant guidance, and thus, require a shepherd. A preacher once said, "Sheep walk with their heads down, nibbling from one tuft of grass to another and easily get lost." My takeaway from this is, if we don't pay close attention to the choices we make and if we move mindlessly from one day to the next, one job to the next, one relationship, one habit, at some point we'll look up and ask, "How the heck did I get here?" Like the sheep, we've nibbled our way to places we didn't ever want to be. It's never too late to take account of where we stand, make adjustment, and re-aim toward a better trajectory.

What we want and what we get depend on how we live *today*.

Three Little Decisions

1.

2.

3.

For Deeper Reflection

How have you allowed yourself to move away from the person you want to be?

If you are not satisfied with the current direction of your life and the choices you've made, on what can you act today that will have far-reaching positive results?

Any relationship we want to have years down the road is being built right now. Consider with whom you can build a stronger dynamic?

---

*Alzheimer's is a tragic disease and affects people in different ways. In a unit I once directed, there was a sweet pastor's wife who was struck with this disease and, as she declined, began to swear like a sailor. Of course, her grown children were aghast and embarrassed about her behavior and said, "Mother never talked like this!" We worked with the family and helped them understand that this was simply part of the disease process, which strips away many social filters, and that behaviors are then often out of the norm.

CHAPTER 6

Discover Contentment

Be thankful for what you have;
you'll end up having more.
If you concentrate on what you don't have,
you will never, ever have enough.

—Oprah Winfrey

"They" Got It All

Many years ago, I wrote a list of people who, it seemed, had more than I did. My list included beautiful women with thin bodies, families who worshipped together, those in careers they loved, those with no financial worries, and those who got to live in Colorado! I kid you not, I had names and personal confirmation that they got more than me!

Why would anyone make such a list like this, you ask? First of all, I'm a list maker from way back, but also, I was on a moaning campaign to God about perceived areas lacking in my life. One thing led to another and there I was, like biblical Job, shaking my fist at God with all my complaints.

"Not fair!" I whined like a three-year-old, "They got more!"

At some point as I shook my fist, a gentle nudge urged me to consider what was true and look more closely at those I'd assumed had gotten it all. Of course, no one gets it "all" and these folks were no exception.

The couple with great wealth and notoriety in the community also had a horrid marriage filled with unkind words and hateful acts. I know this to be true because I sat with them numerous times, attempting to help them get past their bitterness, to no avail. They continued to live behind the brittle façade of outward success, though misery abounded. Certainly that was not desirable!

One day at lunch, the beautiful woman shared about her deep insecurities. She felt judged by her appearance and wondered if people understood she offered more than beauty. Of course, there is nothing wrong with looking our best, but it's never our total package. Even though people looked at her exquisite beauty and sighed, she battled her self-worth every day, believing people summed her up in that one adjective—beautiful. Fortunately, she valiantly overcame her insecurity, spoke freely about it and thereby impacted others who had similar struggles. In our truest moments, we all want to be known and accepted for who we are, not how we appear.

How about the Ivy League graduate—a talented artist with darling kids and a thoughtful husband? Think about the huge school loan, on which she defaulted, due to her out-of-control spending, driving them into massive debt from which they could hardly recover. Her addiction to shopping wreaked havoc on this family. They lost their home and have spent thirty years trying to recoup much of their losses. She lives with the regret of her unfortunate decisions and continues to learn the needed lessons of self-control.

You know those families for whom everything seems to fall into place? The kids are successful in school and sports, everyone likes them, and the mom is president of the PTA. It's easy to feel like *they've scored a sunnier deal until the mother dies in a freak car accident, which leaves her husband and children bereft. It places all else in perspective.*

We may think that if we get the promotion, it'll prove we are better than others at work or that if we win the heart of a certain guy, it will make us feel better about ourselves. If we live in just the right neighborhood or have the biggest group of friends, it will prove our worth. One year in college I tried out for the part of Guinevere in the musical, *Camelot*, and was heartbroken when I only won the part of Guinevere's understudy. In the murkiness of disappointment, I battled all kinds of insecurity about my ability to sing and act and worried what people thought about my *second-place* position. It led to a strong dislike for the woman who got the part and, sadly, I hoped she'd get sick or injured so I could perform the part. Not my proudest response, but jealousy causes some ugly stuff.

A speaker once asked his audience, "Do you feel bitter when others have it better or do you feel better when others have it bitter?" Ouch! Neither of these are nice options. If we find ourselves in either of these categories, we have decisions to make and some work to do on our own levels of life satisfaction. Think about this: *Jealousy comes from counting other's blessings, instead of our own.*

When we continue to compare ourselves to others, we end up either feeling superior to them or incredibly inferior; it's a game impossible to win. Neither of these emotions is healthy. If we have *more* than others, we may think we are superior, but more than likely, we live with a deep fear of losing all we have. On the other hand, if we are the one who feels inferior for any reason, we struggle with our self-worth and believe we are less than what we are meant to be. The dizzy dance with dissatisfaction lands us in a daze as we compete and compare our circumstance to others' and wish for a different life. Let's instead aim for contentment and enthusiastically embrace gratitude for who we are and what we have.

Better than a list of the unfair advantages or a record of those who have more than we do, what if we tried a healthier habit and made lists of the good merits in our life? What if we discovered all the reasons for gratitude and kept our focus there? Let the following thoughts prompt a new list:

- Be grateful our heart continues to beat with not one thought from us. Let's take each breath as the gift it is! How about our eyes, can we see? Do our ears hear? Do our muscles allow us to rise from our bed and walk directly to the coffee pot?

- Consider the inscription engraved on the front of many English church buildings—*Think and Thank*. Think about what we should be grateful for and thank God for any bounty we enjoy.

- Honestly rejoice with the good fortune of others. For example, my grandkids live 15 hours away in another state; my friend's grandbabies live in the same city as she does. I don't always win the battle of envy about this situation, but I'm happy for my friend and attempt to live vicariously through her joy.

- Practice contentment. It takes practice.

- We only have right now! None of us knows what lies ahead. A dear friend of ours kissed his wife goodbye and went for a Sunday afternoon jog. Though an avid runner, he never returned; his heart gave out and he was gone. Find reasons to express gratitude now.

- Be thankful for what we have. What if we woke up tomorrow with only the things for which we thanked God today? It's a sobering thought and reminds us to grow in gratitude.

No one can control everything, but we can accept what comes and stay grateful despite the confounding circumstances.

When our son graduated from the University of Texas, he made plans to move to Los Angeles. He packed every possession he owned into his green Honda Civic and drove through Denver on his way. One night while he was in town, he parked his car in front of a hotel and went to dinner with a friend. When they returned, his car was gone. Stolen. All his possessions were gone—computer, clothes, graduation gifts, camera, and books. Everything was gone except for the clothes he wore, his wallet, and his phone. It took several days for the authorities to locate the missing vehicle, and when they did, it was stripped bare save a few T-shirts on the floor of the back seat. For some reason, the loss of one item in particular was hard for me to overcome. It was a big, stuffed gorilla he had received as a gift when we lived in Germany, and for years it had been a part of our family memories. I know it was only a dumb, stuffed gorilla, but to me it symbolized all kinds of happy times with the kids. I was distressed over the other items he lost, but when I moaned to him about the loss of the gorilla, he smiled and said gently, "Mom, it's just stuff."

Well, that floored me. One, he was right; and two, the wisdom coming from my firstborn was a sober and much-needed reminder. It rings similar to a quote by Marcus Antonius. "If you are distressed by anything external, the pain is not due to the thing itself, but to your estimate of it." I'm grateful my son held this perspective about his things, and I'm especially glad to have learned an important lesson from him.

The apostle Paul, who was imprisoned due to his faith, wrote Philippians 4:12–13: "I know what it is to be in need, and I know what it is to have plenty. I have learned the secret of being content in any and every situation, whether well fed or hungry, whether living in plenty or in want." His example challenges us to make the decision to be grateful even when we're in a tough circumstance. We may be exhausted from working a full-time job while taking night classes, or we're looking for the right spouse but are losing hope. We may have health struggles or are paying off a mortgage that feels impossible or working to lose that last ten pounds (again!).

Satisfaction comes as we face any tough circumstance yet remain grateful for what we have in the moment. Actor Michael J. Fox, first afflicted with Parkinson's disease in his thirties, said, "What happened before, or what may happen later, cannot be as important as what is happening now." The acceptance of who we are and what we have is a healthier approach.

Contentment is learnable. Be satisfied with life today.

Three Little Decisions

1.

2.

3.

For Deeper Reflection

Do you feel bitter when others have it better? Or better when they have it bitter? Decide to move beyond this thinking and be grateful for what you have. Pray for those who seem to have more and for those who are in bitter circumstances. Each life has its share of struggles. Practice compassion.

What would you have today if you only had left what you thanked God for yesterday? Take a moment and express gratitude for all you have. Strive to carry this mindset throughout the day.

CHAPTER 7

Emotional Baggage Check

Try not to react merely in the moment.
Pull back from the situation.
Take a wider view. Compose yourself.
Consider the bigger picture. . . .
Think things through and fully commit.

— Epictetus

Emotion Overload

Paula, a college friend, lovingly helped me battle pesky bouts of insecurity. She endured my emotional roller coaster and gave some needed perspective. One dreary season a jumble of emotions overloaded my brain: I felt guilty, stupid, and worried about several issues.

As we met together for coffee, I expressed uncertainty as to how to move forward and asked for her input. She suggested I dump all my emotions onto the table, and together we would sort out which of them were worthy of all the energy they were consuming.

I drew in a deep breath and dumped the issues, one by one, onto the table. I felt insignificant because a "friend" had walked past and didn't say hello, (petty I know, but it hurt just the same). I struggled with insecurity about my body image and wanted to be in better shape, and I expressed feelings of guilt for poor school performance. It all came out in a rush until there was no more to say. I fell silent and hoped she wouldn't pack up and leave. Fortunately, Paula listened with sincere intention and then addressed the issues one by one. The life lessons she taught that day remain with me still.

She asked some pertinent questions about my situation. Could it be the person who walked past didn't notice me? Might she have been in a hurry or was having a personal crisis of her own? Why was the automatic response about me? Why had her actions caused me to feel small and insignificant? Paula's perspective seemed healthier, maybe the time had come to let go of that overinflated ego and realize other people in this world had issues too!

Takeaway One—*Not everything is about me.*

As far as physical health was concerned, Paula gently said, any anxiety and insecurity never helped anyone get in better shape. All that was needed was a plan and a decision to follow it. Clearly, it was easier to feel badly and moan about the difficulty than to actually do something about it. She encouraged me to develop a workable plan to get in better shape.

Takeaway Two—*Develop and execute a plan that will work.*

Regarding my schoolwork, Paula asked if the issue was a lack of understanding the class material or just neglect? As we discussed it, the truth surfaced; I was not taking time to study, spending too many late-night hours talking with friends, and not getting enough rest. As a result, I was sleeping through early morning classes.

Takeaway Three—*Determine the root cause of the problem and correct it.*

No issues are too much to resolve. But if we give them too much space in our head, without finding a solution or asking for help, we allow those circumstances to determine our emotional state of mind. If we tuck hurt, failure, and disappointment into a dark corner of our heart, these unsettled matters become a dead weight that needlessly drag us down. Because they are difficult to face, it's easy to push them further back in our mind, reasoning it will be simpler to deal with them another day. If we aren't careful, *another day* never comes and the load becomes unbearably heavy, taking a toll on our emotional state of mind and our outlook on life. We call this emotional *baggage*.

Emotional baggage is a mix of emotions we've assimilated throughout our life. When we leave them unprocessed, they begin to pile on and we find the load becoming tough to bear. This is when the experiences from our *yesterday* have a negative impact on our *today*. The descriptions below may help us recognize if we carry unnecessary *baggage*. This is not an end-all list, but if these describe how we respond to day-to-day challenges, it may be time to closely look at what we are carrying. Perhaps we might choose to release the weight or attempt to process some lingering emotions.

- Moody
- Antisocial
- Self-critical
- Argumentative
- Easily annoyed
- Low self-esteem
- Cry for no apparent reason
- Complain and blame regularly
- Pessimistic view of life and the future
- Loss of interest in activities that once brought joy

This is not to say we live like this every day and that we are running around like a Debbie Downer (sorry to all Debbies reading this). But we need to be aware of these tendencies and be willing to address them with this goal in mind: to experience less stress and discover a heightened sense of peace. Part of being human is carrying around life's burdens, but it's up to us to determine how heavy the load becomes. At times, the weight seems to intensify, the emotions muddle and often seem more severe than they truly are. It may be a clue that we are holding on to too much baggage when we overreact to insignificant issues like when someone doesn't hold the elevator for us or we break a nail.

In an article by Dr. Deepak Chopra, entitled "How to Release the Past and Return to Love," the doctor states, "If we've been offended, it may help us to rewrite the offensive story from the viewpoint of the person who hurt us. Pretend to be that person, write what they felt, why they acted as they did and what they now think about it. Follow this, by writing a second account, in the viewpoint of a newspaper reporter telling the story, what they saw and what they understood of the situation. While this is hard work, the payoff is great as it helps us become more objective. It opens our eyes to see more than just our version of the story."

Emotions are not bad or evil, in fact, emotions allow us to experience incredible moments and build meaning into our days. But if left unchecked, some emotions have an adverse effect and drag us down into a dangerous undertow. If we are willing to do the work, to closely examine our reactions, hopefully we'll gain a better idea of how to move forward with them. For me, I needed another person's perspective to face all the emotions threatening to pull me under.

When we visualize the childhood game of leapfrog, we might recognize an important life lesson learned as we played that game. Any leap was greater, higher, and farther when we leaned on the shoulders of others. The same is true when coping with any challenge. When we engage with a trusted friend, allow them to share our load, and genuinely contemplate their advice, it's like the adult version of playing leapfrog!

How grateful we can be for those friends who allow us to *lean* on them for support—those who patiently listen, help us spot irrational responses, and find a more helpful way to think. The takeaways from Paula may help us adjust our frame of mind and release the emotions threatening to weigh us down.

- Remember, not everything is about *me*.
- Develop and execute a plan of action to help achieve success.
- Determine the root cause of the problem and make necessary corrections.

It's up to us to lighten our load.

Three Little Decisions

1.

2.

3.

For Deeper Reflection

Consider ways to lay down our emotional baggage from our past and be free of that burden. Is there an area of failure you are facing? What steps can you take to begin to repair?

Who have you leaned on in times of confusion? Do you allow others to lean on you at times?

CHAPTER 8

Choose Your Own Outlook

The eyes may be the windows to the soul,
but the expression on your face records
each of your fleeting emotions.

—Susan Krauss Whitbourne

Window People

As I stood in the long, twisting line at the San Francisco passport office, it was obvious there would be a lengthy wait ahead. The start of a headache knocked around behind my eyes, and I checked my wristwatch for the seventh time. There wasn't near enough time to wait in line and still accomplish all the tasks on my long to-do list. The crease between by eyebrows seemed to deepen by the minute.

There was nothing to do but endure this nightmare, bide my time, and observe those nearby. One woman caught my attention as she valiantly kept two toddlers occupied. Like a windmill, her arms turned and lifted and protected each of them as they asked for more apple juice, explored under the chairs, and cried over a "boo-boo." She caught the youngest one numerous times, as clearly, he was just learning to walk, and gently called back the older one from wandering too far. The tender smile and pleasant countenance on the face of this busy, young mother was astounding. She seemed surprisingly serene despite the hectic situation—not what anyone would expect.

I don't have to wonder what my faced showed, the aggravation clearly obvious due to the long wait and disruption of my schedule. This was what made the woman with the two small kids even more intriguing . . . was she as serene as her face showed? What secret allowed her to remain composed despite the long wait with her busy youngsters in a crowded government office? Anyone who watched would have understood if she was harried or stern with those little kids, but instead she presented a calm, sweet spirit. This woman remains unknown to me, but she left quite an impression.

When I sense a frown stretching across my face, the composure on that woman's face in the passport office often comes to mind. Or when my eyebrows draw together in annoyance; I attempt like her, to soften my features, lift my mouth into an easy smile and focus on some pleasant thing.

It's amazing how tiny adjustments alter our emotions and bring about a change in perspective. Science tells us, once the *smile* muscles in our face contract, there's a positive loop back to the brain, which reinforces feelings of joy. Smiles are not only cheerful on the outside, but are also expressions our brain uses to tell us we are happy. They also have a social impact with far-reaching consequences. As we smile at others, it may lift their hearts and spirits as well!

Anytime the day is taking a downward turn, remember the woman from the passport office:

•   Find gratitude, even on the tough days—there is always something for which we can be grateful.

- Offer a smile to anyone, no matter how small. Smooth away those furrows between the eyebrows.
- Encourage someone who seems entangled in a hard day. Perhaps God is nudging us to help mitigate a meltdown.

Nelson Mandela in his book, *Long Walk to Freedom*, wrote, "I am fundamentally an optimist. Whether that comes from nature or nurture, I cannot say. Part of being optimistic is keeping one's head pointed toward the sun, one's feet moving forward. There were many dark moments when my faith in humanity was sorely tested, but I would not and could not give myself up to despair. That way lay defeat and death." What a great approach to search for the good in dark places! During the days of apartheid, Mr. Mandela languished for twenty-five years in a South African prison until he was released and ultimately rose to the position of president of his country.

We have little control over the difficult circumstances that take aim at us like a tornado roaring across the plains of Kansas. The tornado might descend in the shape of a short-tempered boss, health challenges, news that disappoints, or insensitive people, to name just a few. And like Nelson Mandela, we recognize difficulties will land in our laps, but the key to our survival is our *perspective* about those difficulties. The only thing we control in any of those unwelcome challenges is our own response.

A Scripture in 1 Thessalonians 5:16 reminds us to "be joyful always; pray continually; give thanks in all circumstances." The idea of finding joy *always* doesn't mean every circumstance we face is easy or pleasant, but instead we attempt to find the joy (the good), in the situation. To do this requires much prayer as we seek to gain God's view of it. This helps us be better equipped to be thankful in all circumstances. In Dallas, I directed a rehabilitation center where we treated a patient who had recently had her right foot amputated. When asked how she was getting along, she responded with a shining smile, "Still kickin', just not as high!" What a joyful spirit she had! If we were in that same circumstance, would we have such a pleasant demeanor? She is a fabulous example of finding the good in a tough situation.

Turn that frown upside down!

Three Little Decisions

1.

2.

3.

For Deeper Reflection

Can you smile right now and release that scowl between your eyebrows? Imagine the joy that will overflow as you fill your mind with gratitude. Do you know anyone in a tough life circumstance who carries a great attitude? What lesson can you glean from them?

CHAPTER 9

Natural Change

> *I am not what I ought to be, I am not what*
> *I want to be, but by God's grace,*
> *I am not what I used to be.*
>
> —John Newton

Taking Flight

Only weeks after my dad died, Tom and I were directed to move to another state to help a struggling ministry. We had to say farewell to our cherished church family in Rhode Island, further breaking my already grieving heart. And we needed to explain to our confused kids why, within a short two-week time frame, we were packing our belongings to move again. All this distress, on top of packing up a house, landed me in an emotional tailspin.

During that tumultuous period, there were several who provided needed help to me, but two women clearly stand out in my mind. As we prepared to move, Vickie Jo joined me in my garden and together we dug iris bulbs out of the dirt. I cherished those bulbs, as years before they had been retrieved from my grandmother's garden, and I was eager to take them along to our next home. A friend who is willing to "get down in the dirt" is a special blessing—but that was Vickie Jo's way. Under the birch tree, we dug up bulbs, wept, and talked about life's funny turns. We shared stories of our children and our dreams. My heart was bruised and raw, and I couldn't imagine how I'd survive the days ahead. But Vickie Jo in her sweet warmth listened and responded with kindness and wisdom. Oh, what a balm for my aching soul!

A few months later in our new city, I helped Betty prepare for the massive undertaking of a garage sale. As we worked, I voiced my concern that I wasn't overcoming my grief fast enough and how I cried at the smallest provocation. She wrapped her long slender arms around me in a warm hug and reminded me that tears are grief doing its work. She suggested it might help to cry as long as needed and as hard as needed and, when my tears were exhausted, to get up and go until the next time my heartache shook loose and my tears flowed, and then do it all again. It was a simple suggestion but one that allowed recovery in a way that was best for me. I loved that she didn't condemn the crying spells but supported and encouraged me—especially since another woman had recently asked if I shouldn't be over this by now! What a blessing Betty was—God brought her along at exactly the right time to help a wounded soul find peace.

Nature, in all its glory, is constantly changing. Whether it is the ever-shifting clouds, the rhythm of sun and seasons, or the birth and death of all creatures. Why is it then that we are so stunned when a big change blows into our life and drives us in an unfamiliar direction? It's like Dorothy in *The Wonderful Wizard of Oz*. One moment this pigtailed girl in a blue-checked pinafore is safely tucked into her farmhouse with her dog, Toto, and the next they are whirled away to the bizarre Land of Oz. Such a sudden and unexpected change may find us stating the famous line, "Toto, we're not in Kansas anymore!"

In grade school, we were introduced to the fantastic concept of metamorphosis. This is when a lowly twelve-legged pest becomes a majestic butterfly. The whole notion seems rather wistful until we stop and consider what takes place for such a transition to occur. The caterpillar wraps itself in several layers of dry casings and then passes through gruesome stages of dissolving and liquefying as it prepares for the big finish. This metamorphosis results in a totally different insect; the creature doesn't just look different, but now has a whole new skill set! With its new powerful wings, it is no longer satisfied wriggling on some branch, but will instead lift off and take flight. Does it have any memory of its dull existence beforehand? The transformation even though difficult, allows that fuzzy earthbound caterpillar to now soar high above the treetops.

Change is a natural phenomenon. Even though we *know* this, change scares us—such as the beginning of a new relationship, becoming a mother or an empty nester, starting a new job, or receiving a troubling diagnosis from the doctor. They scare us because what we knew as *familiar* is changing. When big changes rock our world, how we *morph* through them is central to our ability to *soar above the treetops*. This is why Betty's wisdom was significant. She understood I was going through big adjustments but would, like a butterfly working its way out of a tough papery cocoon, emerge from my grief much stronger.

Another of nature's rare occurrences is the formation of a pearl. The lustrous stone is a natural wonder. But it is nothing more than the oyster's endurance of an uninvited and unwelcome *irritant*. In nature this irritant may be any organic substance trapped inside the shell or most often a parasite that drills through the shell and into the body of the defenseless oyster. The oyster responds by coating the irritant over and over with microscopic layers of nacre. This substance resembles the white of an egg and crystallizes smoothly around the irritant, covering any jagged edges, and over time producing a gorgeous pearl.

When overwhelming circumstances crash in, they feel like an *irritant*, but since we cannot control them, we might instead find a different approach. For example, we might ask, what lesson can be learned from the challenge? Or what new skills have we learned? Have we built a new relationship or grown in our compassion? The answers to these questions are the tender hope that helps us smooth over those rough edges. And like the oyster, after time, the *irritant* can become less irritating. Our journey through a difficult period, our *irritant*, eventually becomes a part of who we are and the story we tell.

A reassuring thought about change is found in James 1:17. It reminds us God "does not change like shifting shadows." Hebrews 13:8 tells us he "is the same yesterday and today and forever." We hold great confidence in this, knowing we can count on God's steadiness and his strong arm on which we lean. His plan for us may not always be understandable or predictable, but his purpose is most certainly trustworthy.

If we resist God's plan, if we refuse to learn and grow, we're like a pear that drops too early from its tree. The pear remains hard and flavorless, never fully ripening to the sweet and tender fruit it was meant to be. God loves us with a perfect love. He remains near to us and will help us grow through any season of change so we might mature into the sweet, tenderhearted women he created us to be.

Let change make us stronger. And wiser.

Three Little Decisions

1.

2.

3.

For Deeper Reflection

What is your view of change—unexpected or otherwise? Do you fear it or isolate yourself when it arrives on your doorstep? Do you believe God is at work in your life to guide you to the place he wants you to be?

What new or reaffirmed skill sets have you discovered from changes you've encountered on your journey?

Name an *irritant* that came into your life that has now become a treasured part of your story.

CHAPTER 10

Rebound Better

*It's easy to be pleasant when life flows like a song.
But the one worthwhile is the one who can
smile when everything goes dead wrong.*

—Ella Wheeler Wilcox

Pinball Pain

*Deep inside I'm hurt. I should let it go, but the hurt lingers. If only
I could understand what my old friend felt, her anger might make
sense. But since she won't talk to me, it remains a mystery.*

*It crashed down a few years back when there was a disagreement
between some work colleagues about which direction to go to move the
group forward. The disagreement grew into a divide and, as divisions
go, became a rift. Each of us was asked to vote on a direction, which
was an incredibly uncomfortable spot, since there were friends in
both camps. Like the choice to walk barefoot over cut glass or red-hot
coals—neither felt safe or desirable. I thought long and hard about
the situation, prayed for wisdom, and cast my vote. My old friend
had chosen the other side and has refused to speak to me ever since.
I called her numerous times (no answer), showed up at her home*

(wouldn't come to the door), and wrote notes, attempting to explain (received no response). Nada. She wants nothing to do with me.

Her severe response is flummoxing; there must be more to it, but it's unclear what it is. It's crazy, because now I struggle to forgive this same woman for her treatment of me! Other friends who know about the circumstance say, "just let it go." They say, some people are unwilling to work through difficulties and refuse to admit any wrong. It's a challenge to heed their words because I'm still hurt and sad to have lost a friend. I miss her.

Most of us are aware of how a pinball game is played. A ball is released out of a shoot, flies through the machine, and briskly bounces off one surface to another, while bells and whistles ring out. The more the ball bounces and ricochets, the more points we earn.

Not so in life. The more we bounce from heartache to heartache, the more our heart bruises, and we experience despair. At times, our emotions resemble this pinball game. Even if the ball has come to a stop, one reminder of an injury inflicted upon us shoots it out, deftly bouncing it against each pain point, as anger and frustration grow with each ring of the bell! Like with my old friend, any reminder of that situation starts the ball pounding. It is difficult to forgive the injury if we continue to relive it.

We're familiar with this saying: "Unwillingness to forgive someone is like us drinking rat poison yet expecting the rat to die." Not a very nice thought, but it means, the harm comes to us! When we bounce and pound on these old wounds, we're holding on to the pain and anger, which is detrimental to our peace of mind. When we tell our frustrations again and again, to whomever will listen, and continue to relive those frustrations, not only does it raise our blood pressure, but those who listen may begin to avoid us due to our negativity. Damage like this takes a toll, it robs us of much joy and peace, and it leaves an ugly scar in its wake.

Consider the story about Lake Okeechobee in south Florida, the second-largest inland lake in the continental United States. It is a backup water reservoir for millions of people, so its levels are carefully regulated. One year, in anticipation of heavy hurricane activity, much of the water was released from the lake. Instead of hurricanes though, a long drought ensued and the water levels in the lake hit record lows.

During this time of drought, a man cruising the shallow lake in his airboat spotted a surprising sight. Stuck down in the muddy soil, exposed by the low water levels, he saw evidence of an earlier settlement. Authorities studied the pottery shards, stone pendants, and arrowheads retrieved from the site and believe these objects belonged to an indigenous people who lived in the lake area over one thousand years earlier. The artifacts are a remarkable discovery and enable us to study the life of these former inhabitants. Had there not been such a bad drought, these treasures might have never been recovered.

Perhaps that's the lesson for us when we go through a rough period. Maybe it's during that time, we'll find treasures we otherwise missed. It reminds me of the adage, *sometimes we fall down because there is something down there we are supposed to find*. If we look carefully, with an open heart and a willing mind, what treasures might be found?

- Increased awareness of those who are true friends
- New friends who struggle with similar issues
- Realization of strengths we hadn't known in ourselves before we went through the struggle
- Acquisition of new skills to help navigate through challenging circumstances
- Newfound wisdom to help us comfort others going through similar situations

- Joy in being able to help others
- Growth of the godly qualities of perseverance, compassion, and patience
- Gratitude for the good days we experience

The lyrics to the song "Bless the Broken Road," recorded by the Nitty Gritty Dirt Band, hits a nerve in us as we are reminded that sometimes good comes out of bad. We can realize the lesson learned or see it as a stepping-stone to move us further down the path. It's as though God uses these life challenges to move us into the places he wants us to be, uses them like signs or markers to bring us to the people he wants us to know. The song closes powerfully with the line, "This much I know is true, God blessed the broken road, that led me straight to you."

What a cool reminder of ways God is at work to bring good out of the bad. It may never be clear exactly happened with my old friend, and I won't know all the pathways or relationships God opened as a result of that painful situation, but I trust He is always at work to move my life in the best possible direction. The choice to resist bitterness and pull away from anger is attainable. The lessons learned in a *drought* are plentiful.

Resist the bounce of that pinball and hold onto any treasure we find.

Three Little Decisions

1.

2.

3.

For Deeper Reflection

Is there a relationship that is *bouncing* you from pain to pain? What one thing can you do today to think differently about that circumstance?

God places each of us where He knows we'll *be our best* and *do our best*—whether we see His hand or not. Think about some "treasure" you have found in the middle of a difficulty. How has God brought you to a better place due to that treasure?

Decisions about OTHERS

Oh, the comfort, the inexpressible comfort
of feeling safe with a person;
having neither to weigh thoughts nor measure words,
but to pour them all out,
just as they are, chaff and grain together,
knowing that a faithful hand will take and sift them,
keep what is worth keeping, and then,
with a breath of kindness, blow the rest away.

— Dina Mulock Craik

The first time I read the above quote it stirred my heart, as I thought about friends who have treated me with such kindness. When friends approach us with respect, reassurance, and sensitivity, we experience a depth of connection that is rare and wonderful. And when we, similarly approach others, we may be surprised at the advent of a vibrant friendship.

I firmly believe God uses our connections with others to help us grow and ultimately to draw us closer to Him. We each have people in our lives who meet different needs, even though we may be unaware at the time what role they play. Some laugh with us at the craziness, while others ask questions that stop us in our tracks. They cause us to look at a notion we hadn't considered before and that is vital to our growth and progress.

And who doesn't love the friend who in everyday conversation mentions positive aspects they appreciate about us? Or those who soothe our souls and help us believe in ourselves again? Some days we only need assistance from the friend who helps us move boxes out of the garage. Such people are worth their weight in gold or at least a gift card to their favorite coffee shop!

Think of that friend who, when we struggle, helps us search to find the good and, if we have lost our way, guides us to trust God again. Hopefully, each of us has a person in our life who is a truth teller, someone who says exactly what we need to hear. They cause us to rethink who we are and how we act. Embrace this friend, this rare relationship, who demonstrates honesty and sincerity.

It is important to acknowledge that not everyone feels they have genuine friends—some feel quite lonely or like they are outsiders. If this sounds close to the mark, take heart—friendships can be built! If the relationships we have aren't healthy or helpful, it may be time to branch out, to meet new people, or to look for them in a different setting. Or it may be time to make the first step at *being* a better friend. Any attempts at being a better friend will only increase the possibility of closer friendships.

Our profound need to be loved is not a modern phenomenon, as clearly depicted in the quote above, written more than 150 years ago. The writer expresses an ache like ours for help, love, and acceptance; she found comfort in having a friend with whom she felt completely safe. It sounds incredibly wistful. What happens though, when we don't have a friend like this? Or what if we do, and conflict arises and threatens to undo it? Those warm fuzzy feelings quickly slip away, and we face heartache and fear.

In this section, *Decisions about Others*, we will examine potential trouble in friendships, possible ways to mend them, and what tactics may work as we deal with interpersonal relationships. Most of us are not *naturally* inclined to look out for anyone but ourself. But as we make decisions to *be* that considerate, caring friend, we may be amazed at the connections we make.

> *Family isn't always blood.*
> *It's the people in your life who want you in theirs,*
> *The ones who accept you where you are,*
> *The ones who would do anything to see you smile,*
> *They love you no matter what.*
> —Author unknown

CHAPTER 11

Communication

*It takes two to speak the truth. One to speak —
and another to hear.*

—Henry Thoreau

Driving "Miss Craisy"

While driving in the car with my preteen daughter, we discussed an upcoming sleepover. I asked my dear daughter if she had telephoned her friend yet, to work out the details . . .

Dear daughter replied, "I just called her."

"Oh, good. What did she say?"

"I just called her."

"Right, but what did she say about this weekend?"

A bit louder now, "Mom, I just called her!"

I knew something had escalated but didn't understand completely what it was.

I replied in my best, soothing-mother voice, "I heard you, honey. What did she say when you called?"

Exasperation now obvious, she responded, staccato-like, "I. Just. Called. Her."

The grip on the steering wheel got a little tighter as did my voice, "Well, if you just called, then what did she just say? Or did you just leave a message?"

Her voice now raised one distinct octave, "Mom! I just called. That's all. I didn't speak to her. I didn't leave a message. I only called!"

Like the sun peeping over the horizon on a summer morning, it dawned on me.

Only called. I released the breath I didn't know I was holding. She was apparently referencing an action. She only called, that's all she did; whereas, I was certain she meant the timing of the call, as in just—it just happened. Fortunately, we didn't come to blows, and eventually we had a good laugh about our inability to communicate over such a small detail in our weekend plans. On several occasions since, we have snickered about our simple lack of clear communication.

At times, we are certain we have said exactly the right thing, but the other person hears it exactly the opposite. Like the time I asked a guest to bring a twenty-pound bag of ice to a party and he showed up with twenty bags of ice! Oh, that was a lot of ice loaded into the back seat of his little Toyota.

Ice is a small thing of little consequence, but what happens when it's something critical, like communication about a flight time, an important business deal, a medical diagnosis, or a sensitive family issue? How as mature individuals do we struggle to clearly and respectfully communicate? At times our anger erupts when someone doesn't seem to *get* what we are saying or if we think they aren't listening. It easily escalates and becomes bigger than it ever needed to be.

How do we stop a simple misunderstanding from intensifying into a nasty disagreement or ugly fight? Here are a few approaches to try:

- Take three deep breaths (in through the nose down to the belly and back out through the mouth) and do a good calming stretch.
- Consider what we said and how it may have been misinterpreted. How might we say it differently, without condescension or adding volume?
- Ask the person to repeat what was heard. When we hear what *they* heard, we may find the tripping point.
- Think about the acronym H.A.L.T. (Hungry, Angry, Lonely, and Tired). When we experience any one of these, it may affect our ability to think with clarity or communicate in a healthy manner. Address H.A.L.T. issues first and then work to resolve the conflict. (Tom sometimes encourages me to eat a little snack because, as he puts it, "You're acting cranky!")
- Consider using this helpful phrase:
  "When you _____ (fill in whatever was said or done), then it makes me feel _____ (whatever is felt because of what was said or done)."

  It's not that they *always* make us feel this certain way, but when they do or say a *particular* thing it causes this reaction. The idea is to help the person not feel attacked or cornered, for what they did or said, but to help them better understand how it made us *feel*.
- Focus on the present. Don't allow past circumstances to cloud the issue at hand.
- Consider the reason for the anger. Might there be other causes escalating the conflict? (Work related difficulties, a bad commute, health concerns . . .)
- Be mindful of body language. When we roll our eyes in annoyance, deeply sigh, walk away, slam a door, or pout, it won't lead to a desirable outcome. Try uncrossing the arms, relaxing the eyebrows, and looking kindly at the person.

- If the conflict refuses to be resolved and heat is rising, consider taking time apart to cool down and reapproach the conversation later. If after this it's still at an impasse, bring in an objective third party to help clear up the confusion.
- Be humble. Admit and acknowledge ways we've messed up.

In the early years of our marriage Tom and I struggled to communicate well. We misinterpreted much of what the other said which then led to disagreements and dark days. Neither of us were very good communicators and our patience and mercy lacked on quite a few levels. At some point, we acknowledged the need for some objectivity and sought out people with healthier marriages for help. We asked questions and spent time with them to observe the dynamics we wanted to imitate. We also read some books on marriage and communication. Together we read chapters out loud and discussed what we learned. It was a significant day when a conflict arose and we resolved it quickly, using our newfound skills. We were both surprised! We were learning how to communicate, how to be merciful and practice patience. It wasn't easy to change our bad habits, and we still made wrong choices. But we grew and were on our way to a successful relationship.

None of us gets through life without some conflict or miscommunication. When a conflict occurs, it's like we've broken a favorite tea cup. Once the initial distress of the damage subsides, we observe the wrecked parts and determine if it is salvageable. If it is, we carefully pick up the pieces and glue them back into place. Almost always the *break* will be noticeable, but it can still be a firm fix and possibly be useful again. It's not dissimilar to the repairing of a relationship. Though resolving a conflict is rarely pleasant, the chance to find a resolution is worthwhile, as we gather the broken bits and with patience and love glue them back together.

Strong communication skills help resolve conflict more rapidly. As does humility.

Three Little Decisions

1.

2.

3.

For Deeper Reflection

What is your typical response when you are in conflict? Do you press in to resolve or pull back and refuse to communicate?

Is there anything from the past keeping you from resolving the present?

As you review the list for ways to resolve a struggle, ask yourself if there is someone with whom you are in conflict and how you might begin the mending process?

CHAPTER 12

Love Smarter

Fake love is when I use relationships for my benefit.
Authentic love is when I give of myself for their benefit.

—Chris Seidman

Touchy, Touchy

"Stop hanging on me, will ya?" The words crushed my high hopes as dad walked through the door from work. All I wanted was to give him a big hug. I wanted him to grab me and throw me up in the air, to have him give me some attention. His rebuff stung and filled my young heart with whispers of self-doubt. Was I lovable? Was I loved?

Dad worked as an electrician and labored for hours in the Colorado cold. When he came home he needed a few minutes to recover, he needed warmth and quiet. He was a hardworking man and provided for our busy family, for which I am extremely grateful. But Dad was tough; he wasn't one to give much reassurance. If I got all As and one B on my report card, he'd ask, "What's with the B?"

Once when Tom and I excitedly shared our plans to move our young family to Germany to serve as missionaries, Dad's lack of enthusiasm was hard to accept. Mom, in her wisdom, later explained it was just Dad's way of saying he liked us living close by. Her words reassured and relieved some of my uncertainty, as she explained he was from that generation of men who did not communicate much emotion nor easily show affection. It was years later I learned more about different expressions of love and better understood how dad showed his love.

While reading *The Five Love Languages*, I learned that we don't all love or feel loved by the same measure. According to this book's author, there are five basic demonstrations of love:

- Acts of Service
- Quality Time
- Gifts
- Words of Affirmation
- Touch

The author, Gary Chapman, lays out the idea that each of us leans strongly toward one or two of these expressions, those that cause us to feel genuinely loved. Our tendency then is to express our love for others by using the language that works for us! But, if another's love language is not the same as ours, then our attempts to express our love to them may not be well received. For example, my top two love languages are, undeniably, touch and gifts. Touch me or gift me and I feel incredibly loved! So to express my love for others, I tend to touch and gift people.

One of my daughters is not naturally a *touch* person. She responds more to acts of service and words of affirmation. When she was a teenager, she would tolerate my attempts to hug and snuggle, but it infrequently came from her initiative. Through no fault of hers, this produced insecurity in my overall abilities as a mom. I mistakenly assumed I had done some great wrong or been too preoccupied when she was a baby. (How many times do we reach into the past and pull out some real or imaginary mistake and attach it to a situation in the present?) After studying Chapman's book, it was clear, we both had different needs and expectations that emotionally fed us.

We made great headway in our relationship as I learned that my expressions of love were not what worked best for *her*. As we discussed the theories in Chapman's book, she better understood what I needed in order to feel loved by her. She now touches my shoulder as she walks by or sits close on the couch because she loves me and wants me to feel loved. By intentionally using my love language, she has made a world of difference in my self-worth as a mom. And I in turn, remember to express with words what I appreciate about her and find ways to serve her. The love then freely flows for both of us.

Dad is gone now. It's interesting to think about his love language. Probably like many men he needed to hear words of affirmation. I needed touch while he needed words. Had we both better understood this concept, I would have expressed all the love I felt for him and he'd have known my need for a hug.

If we find one of our relationships stalled, it might mean love needs to be expressed in the language the other person *speaks*. It's certainly worth a discussion with them to discover ways they feel loved. If we hope to be in a meaningful relationship with this person in five years, ten years, or fifty, it is of great value to determine how this person feels loved and then express it that way. It's also important to discover ways they *don't* feel loved. For example, when we give gifts to someone who doesn't feel loved by a gift (been there, done that), it may have a converse effect—they won't feel loved by us.

Many years back, a friend shared she didn't feel like we were close because we never walked together. This surprised me because I thought we were okay in the friendship arena. But since a walk was important to her and we wanted to be close friends, we walked. What a delight it was to amble along with her, talking and laughing. A funny thing happened in the hours of walking, our friendship grew deeper than we had imagined it could. Over the years we've talked about that turning point and what a difference it made. As we discover what makes our friends and family *feel* loved, the potential for deeper connection exponentially grows.

We never know what a little gesture might mean to another person.

Three Little Decisions

1.

2.

3.

For Deeper Reflection

What is your key expression of love?

Are you in a relationship that is struggling to move forward? How might you determine the love language of that person and better meet his or her needs?

Take a few minutes to write the names of your closest relationships and what it is that helps them believe you love them.

CHAPTER 13

Hear Those Truth Bells Ring

I've had more trouble with myself
than with any other man.

—D. L. Moody

Truth Hurts, Real Bad

I dashed through the kitchen and headed out for the gym when I spotted my daughter's overdue library book on the counter. It had been forgotten, despite my countless reminders to return it to school that day.

I let out a deep sigh as the demon on my shoulder whispered, "Leave it. She shouldn't be rescued. Besides, you're in your gym clothes and not dressed to face other mothers who might be at the school. None of them would show up with their hair shoved into a ponytail."

The angel on my other shoulder said, "Aw, be a good mom and help your daughter. She has a lot on her plate and you've got the time." The angel won the first round. I jumped into my minivan, drove to the school, and parked right in front, since it would take me only a minute to dash in, dodge the other mothers, and drop off the book.

As I jumped back into the car, loud sirens sounded as an ambulance and fire truck roared into the school parking lot. My hand trembled trying to get the key in the ignition and get out of their way. But before I could drive too far, a squad car rolled in, spotted me pulling out of the fire lane and flagged me down. Would this be a friendly warning, I wondered?

The officer strode to my window and said with his slow southern twang, "Ma'am, you were parked in a fire lane. License and registration, please."

After nervously obliging his request, I attempted to argue my case. "We always park here for drop-off, and besides, I was only in there for twenty seconds . . . okay, ninety. I was out of the way in time. No harm, no foul!" The officer stood there in his mirrored aviators, scribbling on his ticket pad, oblivious to my reasoning. I couldn't see his eyes nor seem to budge him from his determination to ticket me.

I tapped my fingers on the wheel as thoughts flew through my mind on how to reason with him. "You know," I began, "I was simply helping my daughter. Do you have kids? Wouldn't you have done the same thing?" Still, this public servant scribbled on his pad and offered no comment. My exasperation was mounting. I leaned out the car window and in my best mother's voice said, "You haven't heard a word I've said, have you?"

The slight nod of his head made me think I might have gotten through to him, which drove me onward. "Do you even understand what I'm saying?" Again, he paused ever so faintly, and I continued imperiously, "I am very concerned about your heart!"

At this remark, he looked at me over the tops of his aviators, shook his head from side to side and handed me the ticket. "Have a nice day, ma'am."

By now, I was both furious and embarrassed at the same time. Furious, because even though I knew I was illegally parked, he would not bend the rules for me, a mother who only wanted to *help her daughter. Embarrassed, because I had scolded an officer of the law. The words just flew out of my mouth, and there was no unringing that bell.*

Truth hurts is a peculiar phrase. Peculiar because truth is a good thing. Shouldn't we want truth in our life? Why is truth at times barely tolerable for us? It's interesting to consider our reaction when confronted with the truth about an area of weakness. We don't always respond well. At times we are stubborn or unwilling to hear the truth, and our pride flashes as swift as lightning. Other times, we become defensive or argumentative because we feel embarrassed that our *truth* is exposed. It's easier to blame circumstances, blame others, or make excuses for our shortcomings. We also experience a fear that others may dislike us when our weakness is exposed.

What if we searched for better responses and allowed the *truth* to help us grow? For example, in the story with the dutiful police officer, about whose heart should I have been *more* concerned? I was the one who was illegally parked in a fire zone and yet did not accept this truth with humility or grace. Although it was not my finest moment, it provided an opportunity for me to face some truth about myself and learn to do better in the future. How unfortunate humility isn't as natural to us as breathing or liking chocolate. What if, instead of being defensive and ungrateful when truth is exposed, we pursued its antithesis—*humility.*

Let's not confuse humility—being humble—with weakness or believing we are *good-for-nothings.* This is only self-abasement. True humility is the absence of arrogance. To humbly face disagreeable truths about ourselves will demand courage and a strong sense of conviction to address the shortcoming straight on. When we bravely face a truth, even though it hurts, it often becomes the best possible time to grow and improve.

One simple act of humility is to give those in our life an open door to *consult* us, to ask their advice or opinion. When we request feedback, it might surprise us what we learn! When we do this, those we ask feel empowered and respected. For example, when we ask an employee for any ideas to solve a work-related issue, it helps them know they are a valuable part of the team. If we ask friends or family for input about some issue in our life, a change we are attempting, or a confusing situation, we will certainly learn some valuable ideas.

This act of asking for and listening to feedback will help draw us closer to people. Keep in mind when we ask for input from others, it's good to consider who they are (their track record, if you will) and to give appropriate weight to their ideas. Not everyone will give us the best solutions or suggestions, but if we listen with humility and respect, we still gain opportunity to grow and learn.

Proverbs 19:20 calls us to: "Listen to advice and accept instruction, and in the end, you will be wise." Wisdom is the great outcome of listening to input from others! There is a man who carries a small notebook in his pocket, so in every conversation, he can jot down relevant points, which he will later review and consider for his own life. What an example of being a constant *learner*, an illustration of humility as he shows willingness to learn from anyone. Whether or not we agree with their input or take their advice, we will most certainly learn something through listening. A quote by the Greek philosopher Epictetus is insightful: "We have two ears and one mouth, so we can listen twice as much as we speak." We can't listen if we are always talking.

When faced with an unpleasant truth about ourselves, let's make every attempt to be humble, to ask for input, to accept what is true and then determine which steps are most beneficial for growth. Imagine a world where we gladly welcome truth and show gratitude for the people who help us to more clearly see ourselves in God's light.

Yes. Sometimes the truth hurts.

Three Little Decisions

1.

2.

3.

For Deeper Reflection

Instead of justifying yourself when confronted with a mistake or weak area, what if you honestly thought about the words said to you, acted on what you learned, and took steps to change?

Do you ask people in your life for their input? Do you believe you're able to learn from anyone? Consider ways you're able to gratefully thank whoever helped you see the *truth*.

Practice Mercy

Teach me to feel another's woe, to hide the fault I see.
That mercy I to others show, that mercy show to me.

—Alexander Pope

Hat Lady

One morning I sat with two of my friends at a local coffee shop and listened as one of them, Audrey, shared a difficulty she faced with her mother. She felt they struggled to move beyond the parent/child dynamic even though Audrey was a grown woman. For example, her recently widowed mom was making decisions about dating that Audrey thought were unwise, and when she tried to discuss it, her mom waved her off with little consideration. Audrey felt disrespected, because her mom didn't treat her like an adult; worried about the consequences of her mom's actions; and was angry at her mom's dismissive attitude. Instead of discussing the concerns further as two sensible adults, Audrey admitted she had pulled away and pouted. (And yes, we all three laughed at the irony in the pouting bit.)

Helen sat sipping her warm coffee and patiently listened as Audrey moaned to us about the inability to reason with her mom and her struggle to unconditionally love her. She longed for harmony in the relationship, but more often than not, she hung up the phone in a torrid of resentment.

Helen wisely told Audrey, "Think of it this way. We all wear distinctive hats as we travel on this road of life. Some hats fit us just right, while others are too big or too flimsy or simply don't match our style. Consider all the hats your mother wears well and be grateful for those. But as for the hats not currently fitting for her, practice patience and love. And keep in mind," Helen paused for effect, "she is your mother."

We sat in silence for several moments and considered Helen's thoughts. Audrey said it helped her understand the unrealistic expectations that her mom, or anyone, should wear all hats perfectly. Audrey realized this was unloving and unkind, and determined to be less critical and more patient with her mom.

Our talents, abilities, and innate skills were determined long before we even knew they were there. We each have amazing strengths. But we must recognize that we also have areas, which are not our strongest suit. Let's admit that not all the hats we wear fit well simply because we place them on our head. Sometimes we must change hats or styles to get the right fit, and sometimes we need time to grow into a particular hat. When we understand this truth, we are able to practice more patience with others and ourselves. When someone disappoints us, or doesn't live up to our expectations, it's helpful to remember this truth and be gracious in our treatment of them.

Consider the wide variety of hats any woman might wear:

- Daughter
- Friend
- Sister
- Wife
- Helper
- Boss

- Student
- Mother*
- Mother-in-Law
- Grandma
- Teammate
- Widow
- Divorcee
- Employer
- Cousin
- Aunt
- Niece
- Homemaker
- Employee
- Coworker
- Servant
- Neighbor

More than likely, some of these hats are worn with pizzazz, while others feel too big or too small. On any given day, a woman simultaneously wears several hats—each one carries responsibility and demands devotion and much energy. (Think how many we are wearing right this moment!) We can't possibly know every issue a relative or work colleague encounters or which hats they are attempting to wear. It's important we give them some slack—let's call it *giving mercy* or *being gracious*. We know our own hats don't always perfectly fit—it's on those days we hope others will show *us* that same mercy.

Mercy: The compassionate or forgiving treatment of someone who we think deserves to be treated harshly; kindness offered to people in a desperate situation.

Graciousness: The act of being kind and merciful.

It's easy to be critical of a friend or relative when they don't handle life the way we think they should. Before offering up our opinions or suggestions about their off-kilter hat, first consider the *health* of this relationship; does it contain enough trust to withstand counsel or critique from us? The following questions may help us know how to proceed:

- Would the help be better received from another source?
- Might there be a more optimal time to discuss the matter?
- How appropriate is it for us to address that hat?
- How would we want someone to address us if the roles were reversed?

If in doubt, *don't.* First take the time to pray and ask God for wisdom. Be still and listen for guidance. Be thoughtful and sensitive in any attempt to help someone adjust their hat. Listen with an open mind, remembering there are numerous ways to handle any given situation. And remember, *when their way is not our way, it doesn't mean it's not okay.* Their way may be the exact right road for them to travel—whether we agree or not.

If we do decide it is appropriate to approach someone—it's best not to put on our *know-it-all* hat, but be humble and willing to hear the other persons' reasoning. We might take our cue from a line of Scripture in Colossians 4:6, "Let your conversation be always full of grace." Be. Always. Full. Not partially or sometimes, but jam-packed full! Does this phrase describe the conversations in which we engage? To be full of grace is to allow other opinions that differ from our own and to be generous and patient with how others wear their hats. Don't get me wrong, there are times when we need to speak up out of genuine concern or say the hard things to those we care about, but it's all in the *how.*

Speaking to someone about a delicate issue is like a turkey sandwich, with the bread of tenderness on each side and the meat of truth on the inside. For example:

Bread: Share what we see as their strengths, tell them what they do well and express sincere admiration for those things.

Meat: Voice our concern and why we think it might be an issue. Ask them to honestly consider our thoughts on the matter.

Bread: End by saying what we appreciate about them and our relationship with them and what we hope for in the future. This is a good time to express the love we feel for them.

This wraps the concern or difficult conversation between positive words of hope and kindness. It's like the time I had a small biopsy taken. While the doctor was injecting the needle into my neck, her assistant stood next to me and patted the back of my hand through the entire procedure. My brain knew I was experiencing pain, but at the same time was soothed by the kind reassurance of the pats.

We can never go wrong with kindness. It will always be the best approach, whatever the issue, whether we speak or write—kind words are never wrong. Most of us are familiar with the saying, "If you can't say anything nice, don't say anything at all." It doesn't mean we should never speak the truth if it might offend, but instead, we express ourselves in a way that honors the sensitivities of others. Show consideration and compassion, no matter how different others' viewpoints are from ours. Look for the good in people and remind them of their positive attributes. This is a genuine way to show mercy and respect.

Search for new ways to show mercy.

Three Little Decisions

1.

2.

3.

For Deeper Reflection

Which *hat* in your life do you struggle to wear? Do you know someone who wears that particular hat well, someone you could imitate or ask for support?

Today, consider someone whose hat choices you have criticized. Have you allowed your *know-it-all* hat to slip on?

How might you practice the *turkey-sandwich* approach?

---

*For those of us who wear the *mother* hat, as our children become adults we experience a significant change. When our kids make the jump from child to adult friend, it is a tough hurdle for them and a chance for all mothers everywhere to practice patience. We hope to protect our kids from pain or trouble, we want them to be settled in good careers and healthy relationships, and secretly, we hope they might live in close proximity to us. Yet at some point they must live their own life—it's a wise mama who lets her children grow into their own hats—even if she doesn't agree with all their life choices.

As my own children grow, I am challenged to find the right balance between pressing-in as a *parent* or wearing my adult-friend hat. It's a delicate dance, so I remind them to be patient, since as we all know, the word mother is smack-dab in the middle of the word smothers! We laugh about this tendency for most moms to smother and hover right in the middle of the mix.

Make a Difference

What you choose today will determine
who you are tomorrow.

—Tim Fargo

Small Things, Big Things

It was obvious. The young woman who stood before me in the
grocery line had little money. Her fingers trembled when she
counted coins dredged from the bottom of her denim purse to pay
the cashier. She licked her lips when she came up short. At first it
was bothersome, this time delay, but it grew into criticalness toward
the woman who had bought more than she should (although truth
be told, it wasn't much of a load).

Annoyed, I shifted from one tapping foot to the other as a
distant memory arose in my mind of a time shortly after college,
when I sat in a similar boat. So tight were my funds, I used every
coupon I could find and carried a pocket calculator in the grocery
store so as not to surpass the twenty-dollar/week grocery budget.
A few times, I too had scrounged through the bottom of my purse
to pay at the checkout, embarrassed to hold up those in the line.
The memory pierced my heart as God's gentle spirit exposed such

a lack of compassion toward this young woman. Who was I to be so unkind and judgmental? I stepped forward and asked if she would allow me to take care of the payment. Unbelief filled her eyes, quickly followed by tears. Her voice shook as she said thanks, gathered up her few groceries, and went on her way. A tentative smile spread across her face.

I'll probably never see her again, but her smile will not soon be forgotten, nor the joy I experienced in overcoming criticalness and helping someone through a rough patch.

We sometimes get caught up in the idea our lives are insignificant, that we don't matter and we can't make a difference from our small corner of the globe. We might think, *One person can't make a difference, so why try? What can one person do?* Such thoughts lead to inaction and may eventually lead to apathy. On the flip side, if we do one small thing, we may find ourselves feeling invigorated, especially when we see a positive consequence.

God created us to care and make a difference to those in our sphere of influence. It was Mother Theresa who once said, "If you can't feed a hundred people, then feed just one." When we help one woman, it may empower her to help someone else who in turn helps another. Each person who helps someone else adds value and joy to the world—it's the idea of paying it forward. As we offer help or support, others may feel inspired to do the same. We may never know who observes our act of service and is then inspired to repeat that kindness along the way.

We don't have to be rich to buy someone a sandwich. We are not too busy to offer words of encouragement. We only need to care. There is a local woman who chooses to do *random* acts of kindness during the Thanksgiving season because she is simply grateful for the life she lives. She places poinsettias on people's front porches, writes notes of encouragement and shovels snow off their cars. Her motivation is to freely share *her* gratitude and joy, but in doing so, she's found it brings incredible joy to *her* heart. Such actions may seem small and insignificant, but anyone who's ever been on the receiving end of such a gesture will admit how it surprises and refreshes. When we serve, whether we pay for coffee for the person behind us in the drive-through or collect blankets to deliver to the homeless, efforts made to help others have a significant impact on our own heart.

As an electrician, my dad often worked in the skyscrapers downtown to light up the city of Denver. A favorite memory he loved to tell was the day he was charged with an important duty. In the very top of the gold leaf dome of the Colorado State Capitol building, the light bulb in the Lantern (a crystal sphere through which the light glows) had burned out. Someone would have to take the elevator to the top floor, go up a flight of stairs and then climb a long ladder to replace that burned-out bulb. How this task came to my dad, we'll never know. Yet he took great pride in the fact he was chosen to perform such an essential task. He understood that few people would ever get to be in the tip-top of the dome, let alone replace the bulb, to shine as a beacon to the city. A light bulb! In the scheme of life, it was a small task, yet to him it was an honorable service to light up the top of such a beautiful landmark.

Little actions have a profound impact. We don't have to make it a chore but simply consider what might encourage someone and do it. As we take the first steps in any act of kindness our heart will fill with joy.

Make a difference, somewhere.

Three Little Decisions

1.

2.

3.

For Deeper Reflection

Have you ever been surprised by a random act of kindness? How did it make you feel?

What do you think about the quote by Mother Theresa—"If you can't feed a hundred people, then feed just one." Who could you serve or help today?

CHAPTER 16

New Perspective

Life appears to me too short to be spent in nursing
animosity or registering wrongs.

—Charlotte Bronte

Reframe Our View

Years ago, a woman at work, Amanda, suffered deep emotional wounds caused by the reckless words spoken by a coworker. For a long time, the two had been friendly, laughed often, and shared a close kinship. Yet after the rash words were said, Amanda refused to forgive the woman who had said them. It disrupted the entire office because she was unwilling to converse with this woman, let alone attempt to resolve the hurtful situation. Most certainly, the coworker who spoke the hurtful words, did so rashly, rather than willfully uttering unkind words.

For Amanda, who had been deeply injured by the comment, anger and hurt feelings were her first reactions. She grew stormy and difficult to approach; resentment devoured her joy. The longer she remained annoyed the more joy she lost. Bringing the matter to a close required numerous conversations to help her reframe her reaction to the inconsiderate words and accept other viewpoints as

*well as a readiness to resolve. It took time for the emotions to calm
and for her to clearly see a better way forward.*

Even though conflict is a normal part of life, not much
unsettles us more than the battle with hurt feelings. We spin
through cycles of disappointment, anger, and sadness or become
stuck in unproductive arguments. Some remain stubborn in their
unwillingness to resolve the issue, while others refuse to see any
point of view other than their own. It's no wonder we struggle in
relationships.

It's baffling how a silly fly flits and taps at a glass window
struggling to get out and continues to smack the same hard
surface, unable to grasp the simple truth—*it will not get out as long
as it continues the same approach.* Likewise, some of the conflicts
we experience may reflect the futility of that fly. As we continue to
hit at the glass pane, we make no progress because we approach
the problem in the same way with the same arguments—and we
end up bruised and tender because we keep hitting on the same
hard issues. We're perplexed as to why we can't seem to get the
relationship *fixed.*

We don't want to take lightly the conflicts we face—they are
most always painful and disappointing. No one denies it's tough
to find resolution and climb out of the rut of resentment. But
what if instead, we turned the conflict on its ear by reframing our
outlook?

From the chair in my office, I see several framed items on
the wall: diplomas, a wedding photo, a state license to practice my
job, family portraits, a letter my son wrote when he was young,
and a picture of my grandson with a broad grin on his face. Such
visuals provide a deep sense of joy and contentment; they represent
accomplishments and those who stand by me on this journey.
Think of which items we place in a frame: pictures of those we
cherish, works of art, scenes of beauty, credentials, and mirrors

(which reflect the beauty of its observer). Such items are placed in prime locations—leveled, lighted, and admired.

But would we frame a photo of our worst memory and place it in a prominent place? Would anyone display portraits of hatred or a certificate of *getting even* on the wall? Why then, do we let the hurts we've experienced hold such prominence in the framework of our mind? Why allow bitterness and memories of a conflict to remain on display?

When we chose to reframe a challenging situation, we still look at it sensibly, but we also look to find different angles or new approaches. The reason someone says or does hurtful things is often unclear—and we may never know those reasons. The hurt they inflicted on us might be intended, but it might just as easily stem from insensitivity or immaturity. (Who among us has never made a rash comment we later regretted?) When we are willing to consider other possibilities, it opens our eyes and helps us frame the circumstance differently.

- Perhaps we'll discover a positive aspect about the person we hadn't noticed before.
- We might see a vantage point to the circumstance other than our own.
- We might realize some good that comes from the difficulty.
- We might have a chance to show mercy toward someone who made an insensitive comment.

When we rise above the fray and give the benefit of the doubt, we find the air up on that high road is much easier to breathe. The point is, we are capable of reframing and responding better than we think. Reframing is more uplifting than when we spend our days moaning about the injustices we've endured. A woman recently told me she struggles every day to maintain a positive outlook in life. She said she needs help to find the good since her first impulse is to see only the negative. We agreed, help is good, but we also understand the choice is *ours* to make. And depending on which we choose, our thoughts become our habits: positive or negative.

Below are some ways we might reframe our perspective and develop an improved mindset:

- Journal. When we put thoughts to paper and read it in black and white, we are able to see clearly and to sensibly sort through the jumble of emotions.
- Make lists of small goals on which to focus. This turns our thoughts toward productive ideas for forward motion rather than being stuck in a negative cycle.
- Write out fifty ways our life is blessed.
- Write out meaningful Bible verses or profound quotes that stir the heart. Write down the golden nuggets of wisdom learned from a friend. These fill our minds with healthier words.
- When facing a conflict, pray and thank God specifically *for that person*. Ask God to open our eyes to their unique journey. This helps us be more compassionate toward the challenges they are facing. Attempt to find positive qualities about them. When we do this in prayer, it helps us keep a more virtuous mindset.
- Sing—it lifts the heart, whatever state of mind we are in—or listen to soul-soothing music.
- Exercise. Go for a walk to help clear the head and enjoy the beauty of nature. This is when we gain perspective on the vastness of our world in comparison to our troubles.
- Take deep cleansing breaths. Think about people who put a smile on our face.
- Take a good, hard look in the mirror and realize, we too have done stupid things and hurt others. (This helps us be more patient when we feel pangs of hurt.)

- Handle those who have hurt *us*, the way we'd like to be handled when we've hurt someone.

When we make this kind of effort, we greatly increase the probability of a reconciled relationship.

I love the word *considerate*. Its Latin roots mean *to examine* or *to deliberate*. If someone is considerate, they put deliberate thought into their actions, based on the need of the other person. It implies one who is insightful and kind in their behavior. Wow! Who wouldn't want connection with a person like that? So an important question for us to ask is this: how do *we* treat the people we meet? Would those closest to us describe us as considerate? Realize it isn't impossible to become more considerate. It involves reframing and refocusing on the positive aspects of life. It means we freely offer kindness, give the benefit of the doubt, listen with sincerity, and treat others as we would want to be treated.

Being considerate may be what is needed to open the window and let that bothersome fly out.

Three Little Decisions

1.

2.

3.

For Deeper Reflection

Can you relate to the fly at the window as you consider a conflict with someone? What hard issues do you continue to hit?

How might you reframe the situation and look at it with a different perspective?

What one thing might you do today to be more considerate?

CHAPTER 17

Second Chances

We are all in need of mercy.

—Dieter F. Utchdorf

Off the Hook

Early in my ministry career, I served as a mentor for dating couples in a local congregation. One young couple asked me to help them build healthy dynamics in their relationship in regard to purity. A few times they admitted, "We slipped up and didn't stay within the moral boundaries we set for our relationship." I counseled them, reminded them of their purity pledge, and spent a good amount of time helping them learn some better ground rules. Yet similar admissions occurred. A belief wrapped itself around my heart—they didn't have much remorse about their lapses.

After another episode, instead of again admitting to me what had occurred, they turned to an older man in our congregation for help who kindly instructed them to recommit their hearts to God's plan for purity and start again. I assume they didn't come to me since they knew I was growing frustrated and would challenge them about their weak convictions.

When I heard this older man had "let them off the hook," I was annoyed with his lack of indignity toward this couple who broke their pledge. Unfortunately, I still envision the scene of challenging this gentle man about his "weak" advice. It is not one of my nobler moments—my words were neither respectful nor kind. Amazingly, he warmly smiled and reminded me how much God loved me and the couple, despite their struggles. It was up to us, as their leaders and mentors, to model God's mercy and patience for them. Much of his kindness was lost on me, as I walked away grumbling, "I don't agree! The couple had not held to the rules!"

Later that day, in retelling my frustration to a friend, he said, "Janet, I wonder if you might think about the verse in Romans 12:3." That stopped me in my tracks! The verse he referenced, "Do not think of yourself more highly than you ought, but rather think of yourself with sober judgment," was exactly what I needed to hear, but disconcerting!

Because of my focus on the sin of others, I couldn't see my own. Thinking I knew better than everyone else blinded me. It wasn't that I didn't care about the older man or the couple—I did care—but I was unable, in that moment, to see the obvious. And yes, the couple did need to develop more self-restraint, but their lacking was not worse than my haughtiness.

Now, at any reference to Romans 12, the memory of the vivid lesson about my arrogance comes back, and I am once again so grateful for the friend who had the courage to speak the truth. Thank God for people who love us enough to speak truth and help us grow to overcome our errant tendencies.

Why is it we plainly and easily see the shortcomings of those around us, but struggle to see it in ourselves? It reminds me of a time someone offended me, which made me mad, which, of course, skews any clear thinking—even on a good day. I was unwilling to forgive the offender, since in my mind, forgiveness offered relief—I was looking for payback. As I spilled the story to my friend Patty, I admitted I was stuck in an angry place but felt, if I forgave the woman who'd offended me, it would let her *off the hook*!

In her soft Louisiana lilt, Patty responded, "Oh Janet. A hook is a terrible place to have someone."

Her simple statement exposed the vivid and gruesome thought of any person who had offended me, hanging on a hook. Of course, she was right. Anger threatens to consume us, unless we find a way to forgive from the heart. More than likely, the person we've placed *on the hook* doesn't even know it or care that we are angry! They are probably skipping through life in a meadow of flowers, unaware of our misery while we trudge through the tar pits—knee-deep in the goop. The reality is, when we keep people on a hook, we also keep ourselves on one.

James 1:19-20, cautions us to "be . . . slow to speak and slow to become angry, for man's anger does not bring about the righteous life that God desires." Which best describes our reactions? Are we slow or quick to become angry? Often, when we're hurt, it's difficult to follow this practice. Anger easily blinds us to what is true and escalates our troubles.

Being blinded to the truth is similar to kids playing hide-and-seek in the neighborhood after dark. I remember how we hollered and squealed with delight until the shadows of swaying trees and rusty trash barrels began to resemble ominous creatures lurking in the dark. We weren't sure what was out there and our imaginations went into overdrive. Similarly, angry emotions distort our thinking. If we aren't careful and only respond to hurt feelings with anger, we may then begin to accept the wrong beliefs, such as:

- We believe, if we hold the one who harmed us *on a hook*, they will understand the pain they've caused us.
  They won't.

- We think too highly of ourselves and believe we know better than everyone else.
  We don't.
- If we stomp our foot in anger or pout, we will feel better.
  We won't.
- When we hold the pain close and allow it to fold around us like armor, it will protect us from future pain.
  It won't.
- When we remain unwilling to yield, we believe it shows strength.
  It doesn't.
- If we admit our fears, people will think less of us.
  They won't.

Do any of these beliefs truly make us happier? Do such reactions develop meaningful relationship dynamics? We already know the answer. It's only natural at times to experience hurt and disappointment from people. But the choice of how we respond lies solely in our court. Will we respond with anger, bitterness, and resentment or be gracious, forgiving, and *let people off the hook*? Keep in mind, letting someone off the hook is *not* saying we ignore the hurt or stick our head in the sand, but rather, it's about how the hurtful circumstance ensnares us and we struggle to move past it. It cannot be overstated—the choice to respond graciously when we are affronted, is ours.

A big part of this graciousness begins when we purposefully take a long look in the truth-mirror *before* pointing out the wrongs of others. This is a time to closely observe our own reactions, to make sure our anger isn't blinding us. It reminds us we've all made mistakes and are capable of hurting those we care about. When we realize this truth and accept it, we'll be more prone to offer this grace to others, because we understand we are all in the same boat of desperately needing mercy!

Consider this helpful thought from the book *Forgive for Good*, by Frederick Luskin: "Each of us moves from forgiveness to healing—not from healing to forgiveness." Forgiveness is us being gracious and merciful. It is us letting someone *off the hook*, not because they have done no wrong, but because they, like us, need mercy. It's us not reacting with anger but with patience and kindness. For each of us, deciding to offer up grace and forgiveness is what starts us on the road to healing and emotional health.

We can't wait to be healed before we choose to forgive!

Three Little Decisions

1.

2.

3.

For Deeper Reflection

Is there anyone right now whom you won't let *off the hook*? Is there someone you want to forgive, but struggle to do so? What will it take to make that first step and offer mercy?

Which *wrong* beliefs have you held onto for too long? What are some better beliefs to hold onto?

What is one step you are able to make to move toward healing?

CHAPTER 18

Value of Appreciation

Appreciation is the highest form of love.
It is the type of love that can blossom
even when it's not returned.
Appreciation asks for nothing and gives everything.

—Dan Baker and Cameron Stauth

Bossy Cow

Once while I was overseeing a large ladies' luncheon, there was still much to be finalized, yet our start time was drawing near. Volunteers were scurrying all over the reception hall like ants at a picnic, but in my view of it, not quickly enough. Not realizing I did it, I pulled out my "bossy hat," placed it firmly on my head, and began to push those volunteers, left and right.

Theresa, the woman in charge of the decorations, touched my arm and whispered in a hushed tone, "Janet, I know we're short on time, but maybe you could take a minute to thank these women. They are volunteers and many have been here since early this morning. Maybe you could let them know how much you value and appreciate them." With her smile and one raised eyebrow she knocked that bossy hat right off my head!

I was pinned to the wall and there was no wriggling out of her clear intimation! I had been pushy and rude with these good-hearted women, and she called me on it. Only someone with a huge ego would think they could pull off such an event without the support of many helpers. Each woman brought a special talent, which collectively made the event a success—altogether a mighty army of ability! I was grateful for them but needed to do a better job showing my appreciation.

The simplicity of this saying rings true: "Some people come into your life for a season, others for a reason." It seems that God sends certain people into our life to point us a certain direction or help us learn valuable lessons. Theresa was a friend in my life for only a season, and if we never meet again, she taught me an important lesson, one I attempt to remember whenever I'm directing any group—*my words matter*. Appreciation matters.

In fourth grade we used the term, *Bossy Cow*, when we didn't like someone telling us to do something we didn't want to do. I suppose no one likes to be bossed, even though at times it's a necessary negative. The secret to being a good boss is in knowing *how* to direct others. The tone we use and our choice of words will greatly enhance our effectiveness in relationships. We've all known people who have that little edge in their voice every time they open their mouth. Is it really how they feel (edgy) or has it simply become a bad habit? Picture a three-year-old who says, "It's my dolly—give it back!" Are you able to hear her tiny voice that puts far too much weight on *each* word? Now, put that toddler's voice in an adult: "Don't sit on the couch! I just fluffed the pillows!" Or "Get that report to me by the end of the day!" Or some woman at the deli counter who shrills, "I was here before her!" Ugh! When (not if) we hear this voice coming from our own mouth, it might be time to stop and ask what is at the root of our tenseness? Has it simply become a bad habit or is something deeper causing the bitter-sounding edginess to gush out?

When we think of snarky remarks we've made or as soon as they come out of our mouths, we feel immediate regret. But there is no pulling those words back out of the air—it's like trying to unscramble an egg! Oh yes, our words matter. We should take stock of how we talk and the words we choose. The Bible speaks to the power of our words in James 3 as it parallels the tongue— such a small part of our body—to a spark, a spark hot enough to set a whole forest ablaze! The tongue causes troubles aplenty!

Before we point a finger at the hurtful words *others* have said, let's first take a close look at ourselves. Check out this list, do we allow such words to escape *our* mouths or define us?

- Reckless
- Insensitive
- Deceitful
- Gossipy
- Undignified
- Unforgiving
- Faithless
- Crude
- Demeaning
- Slanderous
- Negative
- Argumentative
- Patronizing
- Arrogant
- Screaming
- Angry
- Ungrateful
- Bossy, as in the example above.

Wow! Not the words we'd ever want used to describe us. Nor do we want to spend time with people who behave in such a way. If these types of comments come out of our mouths, how do we expect to build meaningful or lasting relationships? None of these words encourage, build up, or show appreciation—instead they do quite the opposite! Think about this phrase: "Say what you mean, mean what you say, but don't say it mean." As we look at our approach to relationships, realize our words are key to enjoying successful interactions.

When we read the prayer in Psalm 19:14, we hear King David say, "May the words of my mouth and the meditation (thoughts) of my heart be pleasing in your sight, O LORD." He says this prayer right after asking God to discern his errors and forgive his faults. We cannot know which faults he is referencing, but his great desire was for his thoughts and words to please God. It's a noble prayer and a good one to imitate. It stands to reason, if our thoughts and words please God, they will also have a pleasant effect on those around us.

When someone compliments us, encourages us, or reminds us of the good we've done, we stand up a little straighter and believe we're capable of just about anything. If our act of service is recognized, our chest fills with pleasure, it stirs us to do *more* good! We love it when others speak to us like this, but do *we* compliment and praise others? Do we speak freely about our gratitude and appreciation?

Let's take a minute to consider what might happen if we permitted only pleasant or friendly words to come out of our mouth. Imagine how our *hearers* will feel when those words reach their ears. They'll smile and be filled with joy. Their eyes will brighten with hope and faith that what they've done matters. Many will wrap us in a warm hug of gratitude. What if the words of support and strength we spoke were exactly the nudge they needed to not give up that day? Imagine a world where this is the norm! Such words demand little, yet soothe hearts like tea with honey. If it is our aim to grow healthy interpersonal relationships, our words will need to be carefully weighed.

Appreciation is a wonderful gift that costs us very little.

Three Little Decisions

1.

2.

3.

For Deeper Reflection

In which ways do you tend to be bossy or controlling? How might you change your approach and use different words to convey your expectations?

Review the list of negative words above. Which of them could be used to describe your words? What steps can you take to make better word choices and build more harmony in relationships?

Who do you know whose words are filled with gratitude and positivity? How are you able to imitate them?

CHAPTER 19

Right Response

You are responsible for your life.
You can't keep blaming others for your dysfunction.
Life is really about moving on.

—Oprah Winfrey

Unresolved

Once at a national church conference, I ran into Barbara, a woman with whom I'd had a parting of the ways, due to her inconsiderate behavior toward me in a public manner. I was astonished at how fast the pain of that memory surged, and I was just as astonished how minute details of that exchange arose in my mind as if it had happened yesterday instead of years before!

But Barbara greeted me with a big smile and said it was good to see me again. Good to see me? Who was she kidding? Had she forgotten how things had ended? My mouth could not form any words, although I'm sure I murmured some kind of politically correct response and then half ran away. Deep inside there was a rumbling, like a volcano about to blow! How could I have such a visceral reaction to someone I hadn't seen for years? Because

Barbara lived in different state, because it had been years ago, I thought the whole nasty incident was over.

But nope, it wasn't. Our issues were not resolved but had been stuffed into the back of a basement closet. Clearly there was much to reflect on and pray about—the intensity of those feelings was confusing. Once my heart rate slowed, I evaluated the curious reactions and accepted there was still some work to do when it came to the subject of conflict resolution and forgiveness.

When we experience physical pain, it shoots forceful signals to our brain; it robs us of breath and narrows our vision. It renders us unable to think about anything *but* the pain. Emotional pain isn't so different. When someone emotionally hurts us, our mind zeros in on the injury, as we try to grasp why and how it happened. If we remain focused solely on the pain, and make no effort to repair, it's easy to fall into a dingy hovel of misery.

The following four reactions are common responses to misery and threaten to keep us in that dark place. Here is what I *reasoned* in my distress with Barbara:

1. If only

- If only I had handled the situation differently.
- If only we hadn't run into each other.
- If only we had resolved the issue long ago.

Really, such thoughts never resolve the hurt. It is futile to think like this since a bell will never be unrung. *If only* is a helpless form of regret and is useless in moving us toward reconciliation.

2. Blame others

- Barbara is the reason for my discomfort and bitterness.
- Barbara should not have said it was good to see me.
- Barbara should have not talked badly about me.

Such constant accusations not only extend the damage in relationships, but it keeps us from learning important lessons about ourselves. It ultimately robs us of joy. We wrongly believe that if we condemn others in our blame game, it will soothe our wounded heart or make us feel better about our wrong reactions.

3. Demand answers

- Why did Barbara hurt me all those years ago?
- Who started it?
- Why do people hurt me? (Does anyone hear the foot stomping?)

As long as we focus on the behavior of others, we don't address our own. Even if we know why or where the hurt originated, it will not help our heart to heal.

4. Become apathetic

- Try not to care what Barbara thinks (*Whatever!* We say with lifted eyebrows).
- Avoid the person and the situation.
- Push the memory away and try not to think about it. Act like things are fine.
- Throw up my hands and quit trying.

These responses to our difficulties may seem like the easier options, yet they prevent us from building and maintaining meaningful relationships. And like the story with Barbara, such issues always resurface. Always.

A Better Question

Sometimes in the confusion of emotion we moan and ask, "Why me? Why did this happen?" But since none of us is able to explain *why* certain things happen or *why* people act the way they do, then *why* do we ask? No one ever receives an answer to such a question. What if instead, we asked a better question, such as, "What might be learned from this situation?" This response shows we understand life has ups and downs, and if we'll embrace them, we may gain understanding and wisdom.

And perhaps an even better question is this: "What is my best response to this situation?"

The great thing about asking the right questions—we'll know the right answers almost every time!

We are always responsible for how *we* act and react, no matter how we feel. For example, when we react to an offense with anger or bitterness, that's on us. We are the ones who are angry, the ones who are pouting and the ones who are bitter. No one *makes* us react in an angry or bitter way. It's our choice. And the good news is since we are the ones reacting, we are the ones who are able to *better* react.

Just knowing that forgiving someone is the right move is not the same as *actual* forgiveness. As always, the *knowing* and the *doing* are quite different. Even when we understand how beneficial forgiveness is to our emotional health, many of us stagger and falter as we attempt it. We spin in a guilt cycle because we *know* it's right to forgive. But since we're unsure how to approach someone to resolve an injury, or we feel so hurt by it, we cannot bring ourselves to do what we know is right.

Other times we (falsely) believe we are justified to hold a grudge because certain hurts are simply unforgivable. Also, not everyone will accept our attempts to forgive or be willing to reconcile with us. At times, we may need to *agree to disagree* about a situation. At other times in this struggle to forgive, we might ask a trusted friend or a professional counselor for help, allowing them to guide us toward healing in the relationship. Some situations are not easily unscrambled. It will take time and patience, and prayerfully, our efforts we will lead to peace and resolution.

Forgiveness can be complicated and thorny. Like when I harvest raspberries in early fall, I see the tender fruit tucked back in behind the bright green leaves and long to taste their sweetness, but first I must navigate those thorns that prick my fingers.

The fruit of resolving a conflict is always worth the sting of the thorns. Always.

Three Little Decisions

1.

2.

3.

For Deeper Reflection

Are you spending too much time saying, *if only* and *blaming* others for your pain? How might you ask the right questions and respond in a better way?

Who is someone you need to forgive? Could you choose a better response to some emotional injury that has squarely landed in your life?

CHAPTER 20

Please People, Please

Remember, you can't make everyone like you.
If you pretend to be someone else,
you will attract the wrong people.
If you choose to be yourself,
you'll attract the right people
and they will be your people.

—Pia Edberg

Is Anyone Listening?

I had just buckled up and turned off my cell phone, as I readied for the long flight from Boston to Denver. Everyone on the plane was settling into their small space, scrutinizing those sitting to their left and right, and establishing who was going to maintain control over the armrest. Some of them had their nose in a book; others were asleep or fiddled with a laptop. Kids bounced on their parent's lap as we all anticipated takeoff.

A pretty flight attendant, with her black hair tucked into a tight bun, stood at the front and began the typical safety demonstration in a professionally trained voice—the same presentation anyone has heard over and over if they've flown much. At that point our eyes glazed over and most everyone tuned her out. Yes, we know there is an instruction card in the back of the seat in front of us. Of course, our life jackets are tucked securely under our seats and who doesn't know that if we are traveling with someone who needs assistance, we put on our oxygen mask first before we help them get theirs. Yes, we've got it. Yes, yes.

Looking around the plane, it struck me how few people paid attention to her instructions, even though she was doing her best to assure us we would be safe should anything happen during the flight. The thought crossed my mind, How terrible, no one was listening. *I assumed she felt insecure about this—since, if I were in her shoes, I might. That's when I set out to make sure she* felt *heard by sitting up straight and craning my neck so she'd notice my rapt attention. With my eyes riveted on her and nodding to all her comments, I did everything in my power to communicate to this poor woman that her instructions were not unappreciated. At least one person on this plane cared; she could count on me to be a stalwart passenger.*

Was her happiness really up to me? Of course not! Who knows why it mattered to try so hard, but my best guess is this: I wanted her to think well of the nice lady back in 17C. It's such a stupid way to think. Really, was that flight attendant any happier? Certainly not due to my actions. And if honesty comes into play, less of it was about helping her feel appreciated, and more was about self-absorption—of hoping she had a positive image of me. Me.

The dictionary doesn't list a definition for *people-pleasing* nor does the thesaurus offer suggestions for synonyms. It's a modern phrase that carries a negative vibe; tossed around in society implying someone has ulterior motives, is a pushover, or is unable to think for themselves. If we wrote a definition, it might be:

a deep consuming desire to be *liked* by everyone; a belief that we must think and act the way other people want us to think and act.

It's like the time I was flossing my teeth and hoped my dental hygienist would be proud of the good job I was doing. What? Was my motivation to floss simply to fish for a compliment at the dentist? How about the motivation to have healthy teeth? Again, too much *me* in the picture.

Or it might be that someone is trudging along pleasing people due to some sense of *obligation*. Like the woman who declared she would never again entertain dinner guests. To a casual observer, it may sound callous. But this woman had been a corporate wife for over 30 years, and as such, it fell to her to throw elaborate dinner parties for her husband's rich clients, which included gourmet meals, a professionally decorated home, and an ever-present smile. Even her immaculately dressed kids and perfectly groomed toy poodle knew to behave! It was her job and she did it well, but it took a toll and wore her out to always be on display. She was pleasing those people, yes, but at what cost?

At first glance, the phrase *people-pleasing* doesn't sound too bad . . . pleasing people—it has a nice ring to it. When we go deeper though, we recognize people-pleasing is an oxymoron; it is less about the people, less about pleasing them and much more about *us* hoping they will like us if we please them! Being consumed by this need to please can be exhausting. We worry over peoples' thoughts about us—and bend over backward to gain their approval. A woman once said, "I'm a recovering people-pleaser." When questioned about her comment, she admitted she would always be recovering since her tendency to please people was a deeply ingrained behavior—and thereby an ongoing process to overcome.

What could be the basis for such struggles to please? Did it start at a young age when we internalized the positive reaction we received as we complied and pleased people? Are some personalities simply more prone to seek and long for acceptance? Based on how we were raised, some sincerely believe it is the right thing, this *aim to please*. Others struggle to say *no* to some request, because the disappointment in the eyes of the asker is too much to bear. Even if we are able to exhibit some backbone and say the dreaded *no* word—we then spend days shrouded in guilt or worry about the person's displeasure with our response.

Whatever the reasons, the core issue seems to be our desire for others to think highly of us and be impressed with our efforts. At the end of the day, this type of people-pleasing emerges as somewhat problematic. It gets in the way of building healthy connections, since we get too caught up in how we *think* they feel about us, rather than how they really do feel about us.

Sometimes we struggle to find that quirky balance between a deep desire to please people and the other extreme, not giving a flip what anybody thinks. Do you know someone who says, "I don't care," a bit too much? Picture a large pendulum swinging back and forth over a center point, which represents healthy interpersonal interactions. When it swings too far to one side, we find our cynical selves, not caring if people are pleased or not. When we are at this point, we do whatever we want, which in its extreme form appears derisive toward others or indifferent. When that same pendulum swings back to the other end of the spectrum, we may find ourselves overconsumed with what people think about us and pour all our energy into their opinions.

| Overconsumed people pleaser | → | Perfect balance | ← | Unconcerned and apathetic to others |

When we find we've swung too far to one side or the other, hopefully we will sense our extreme reaction and back off a little to re-aim for that perfect balance in the center. This process takes intention and practice.

The following approaches may help us find that balance:

- Learn the difference between pleasing someone based on our frantic need to find approval or pleasing someone based on a genuine desire to help.
- Find healthy ways to move beyond the unremitting worry of what people *might* think. The truth of the matter is this; we have zero control over anyone's thoughts besides our own.
- Decide not everyone will like us or everything we do. Be all right with it.
- Take a bite of courage and consider the true motivation for pleasing certain people. Don't run the risk of becoming a manipulator by using your ability to please. Remember the despised teacher's *pet* in school or that colleague who is always angling to get the ear of the boss.
- Don't let someone else's low opinion of us become *our* opinion of us. Our self-esteem should be *internally* generated and need not be affected by the opinions of others. Our value is not in what others think, but in who we believe we are in Christ! Of course, we don't mind when others think well of us, but the bottom line is—what *we* think and believe about ourselves matters more!
- Read books or listen to podcasts about how to set limits and appropriate boundaries. This may help us develop healthier relationships. Know it's okay to say *no* at times—it doesn't put us on the *slacker* list.
- Believe, with absolute certainty that it's *not* okay for someone to take advantage of our time, our emotional stamina, or our good-heartedness.

Living this delicate balance is like learning the *Cha Cha*. One-two, one-two-three, one-two, one-two-three . . . Toes are stepped on, turns go the wrong way, and the beat gets lost—it takes tenacity to learn this skill. But the choice remains: quit or keep trying to learn the steps! Life in the people-pleasing balance is not dissimilar to this. At times, we will step on toes and feel clumsy; but we learn, we adjust, and we find ourselves building vibrant connections with those people who mean the most to us.

So yes, let's please people! Let's please the people we love, the people we truly want to encourage and support. But let's reign in the pleasing of people that causes unnecessary stress and worry.

Imagine our world if each of us practiced a balanced approach in pleasing others.

Three Little Decisions

1.

2.

3.

For Deeper Reflection

How might you *please* someone in a healthier way today? Consider the pendulum and find one way to move closer to the center balance.

In learning the *dance*, even though you may step on toes, how can you move yourself forward in a positive direction?

CHAPTER 21

When Friends Hurt Us

How wonderful it is that nobody
need wait a single moment
before starting to improve the world.

—Anne Frank

Stupid Monkeys

People say I'm a people person—the more people, the better! When there is a void of interaction with a lot of people, I get emotionally tied up in knots. My safety net is to initiate—call friends near and far, reach out across the miles with letters and cards, and organize times together. But sometimes I wish friends would reach out to me. Sure, many of them return calls or emails, but few of them actually take the initiative.*

Once while whining to my sister Marty about these friends of mine who don't initiate, I told her it was tempting to not call them or reach out anymore. With my arms crossed and my neck bobbing like a Christmas turkey, I said, "And then we'll see just how good the friendship is!"

My sister gently nudged me and said over the top of her readers, "I think you need to remember something. Connecting with people is a gift God gave to you—it's a strength and one of the things people love about you. Your gift is like a glue that holds people together!"

Still miffed at my friends, I harrumphed at this, unconvinced by her words. She then reminisced on an important lesson she had learned. Over many years she had hosted countless people in her home for a meal, but rarely did those same people return the favor. This situation used to bother her—a lot—until one day it occurred to her that the ability to be hospitable is the gift God gave to her! He gave other gifts to other people, but to my sister he gave generosity and hospitality. She decided to be okay with her gift and use it the best she could. After she had this "eye-opener," she used her gift with much more freedom and joy.

She went on to explain that our spiritual gifts are God-given and to encourage me to not hold mine back but instead to use it to build cherished and meaningful relationships.

I love the Message Bible rendition of Galatians 5:22–23, speaking about the gifts God gives:

> *What happens when we live God's way? He brings gifts into our lives, much the same way that fruit appears in an orchard—things like affection for others, exuberance about life, serenity. We develop a willingness to stick with things, a sense of compassion in the heart, and a conviction that a basic holiness permeates things and people.*

God has given each of us unique qualities, pieces of himself—pieces of holiness, to use in this life to build up others, to help and encourage many. My sister's wisdom is humbling and her gentle teaching about God's gifts still echoes in my mind. What a wonderful reminder to let go of insecurity and not to grasp disappointment with such an iron fist.

There is a story about Spider Monkeys (aptly named for their long arms, legs, and tail), who dwell in tropical jungles, and the ease with which they are caught. The trapper carves a small hole into the side of a large gourd and fills it with berries, which the spider monkeys love. The monkey squeezes its hand into the small opening of the gourd and is unable to draw it out due to its fist now filled with the fat berries. The trapper simply grabs the monkey and the hunt is over. It's that easy. If the monkey would only loosen its grip on the fruit, how easily it would gain its freedom. And we think—the stupid monkey.

The parallel between these monkeys and us is closer than we may want to believe. When we hold tight to hurt and disappointment, we, like the monkeys, are easily taken captive by bitterness and resentment. If we want to avoid being captured, it's imperative we find quick and healthy ways to loosen our grip on those "berries."

To sort through the jumbled emotions of hurt and disappointment, try the following exercise:

- Divide a piece of paper into three columns.
- In the left column, name the emotion nipping at our heels.
- In the second column, what triggered those feelings?
- And in the third column, list what is true?

For example, my feelings were hurt because my friends were not initiating, so I named the emotion, thought about the cause, and worked to focus instead on what was true:

What is the emotion?	What caused the emotion?	What is true?
I feel hurt and angry.	My friends don't call often. I am the one who usually initiates.	I've been given the gift of initiating. Others may not have this same gift.
I feel sad.	I think no one considers my needs.	I have friends who love me.
I feel lonely. I don't like to be lonely.	I have stopped reaching out to my friends.	Remember, God never pulls away.

To face our emotions in *black and white* sobers us, but when we take a little time to be honest about these emotions, the truth of the matter will come into focus. As we read the third column a few times and attempt to align our emotions with those truths, we'll find it easier to let go of the "berries" we're clutching from column one.

Christian author, C. S. Lewis, wrote, "Getting over a painful experience is much like crossing monkey bars. You must let go at some point in order to move forward." It takes courage to let go of the bar, rather than clinging with white knuckles to a hurt inflicted on us. We can release our grip on that bar and move on to the next. It's our choice to move forward.

Our choice—our steps.

Three Little Decisions

1.

2.

3.

For Deeper Reflection

How might you let go of the "berries of bitterness" that hold you captive? What *truth* can you discover that will help you push past the jumble of emotional reactions? How might you better act on this truth?

Stop and take stock of the gifts God has placed (for a reason) in your life. Consider how you can use those very gifts to build meaningful relationships.

*Disclaimer to friends who say, "Wait a minute, Janet. I *do* call!" Yes, true—but this is an attempt to own and acknowledge my insecurity here. To those friends who do call and do care (you know who you are), for you I am deeply grateful!

Decisions about OUR SELF

It is not what you are that holds you back.
It is what you think you are not.

— Author unknown

Is there anyone we know who doesn't want to improve herself in some way? It seems that everyone makes comments about a desire to change or make progress. In January, we are inundated by New Year resolutions—it's as if it's in our winter DNA to strive for betterment. And even though each of us *hopes* to grow, too often those hopes and ambitions are swallowed up in doubt, and we are left to wonder if we will actually make headway in this self-improvement arena. We struggle to believe we will accomplish what we set out to do, and it hampers our progress.

At a morning devotional group, I heard a speaker share the words of Jesus: "Love the Lord your God with all your heart and with all your soul and with all your mind. . . . Love your neighbor as yourself" (Matthew 22:37–39). In reference to this passage of Scripture, the typical question often asked is this: how can we truly love our neighbor if we have so little love for ourselves? It's a fair question, but on that day, our speaker added an interesting twist to our struggle with self-love. She said, "Stop bullying yourself about every little thing!"

Her comment caused me to lean forward in my chair, as I considered this fresh perspective on such an endemic thought. I was struck with her admonitions to stop the negative talk, to stop believing the worst, and to learn to love the way God loves. With utmost certainty, I know I am *not* alone in this battle against rampant self-bullying, against those voices in my head saying, *I'm not good enough, thin enough, strong enough, or spiritual enough.*

Negative self-talk can derail us even on the best of days. Our tendency to be self-critical (to bully ourselves) overshadows our confidence, and the damage is impossible to measure as it blows in those evil triplets of self-doubt, insecurity, and uncertainty. Overcoming these voices involves a decision to disembark from that Bully Express and board a different train of thought. As we toss those negative voices overboard and learn to *think in a different way*, we are better able to accept the truth about God's amazing mercy, to see how he cherishes us, and to realize he remains by our side through every struggle. It's powerful stuff. As we acknowledge these truths, it's like we've harnessed the incredible power of a locomotive—it advances us far down the track of confidence and self-assurance!

In this final section, *Decisions about Our Self,* we'll closely examine our confidence and see why it matters. First, we'll establish how God views us and what he longs to see *in our heart.* Then we'll look at some unhelpful or self-destructive habits we too easily tolerate—those very habits which prevent us from rising to the level of our *best* selves.

The aim of each chapter is to provide us with courage to move beyond insecurity by making small but good decisions, which propel us forward. Those small steps will help us increase in our self-confidence, and before we know it, we'll find our overall outlook is beaming as brightly as the noonday sun.

> *Only as high as I reach can I grow,*
> *only as far as I seek can I go,*
> *Only as deep as I look can I see,*
> *only as much as I dream can I be.*
> —Karen Ravn

CHAPTER 22

God's View

Accepting God's love involves a relentless
hushing of voices that whisper otherwise.

—Philip Yancey

Value of a Twenty

Years ago, Tom and I had the great honor of leading Christian teen ministries. The teen years are such a perplexing time of life, and so with this age group we needed to find creative approaches to teach and to help them gain perspective.

One young girl had a difficult life story—she and her family had been wrecked by heartache and violence. She had been mistreated and assaulted, which landed her in a few foster homes, and she was then moved to live with unfamiliar distant relatives. I met her when these relatives brought her for a week at the summer church camp I directed. My first impression of her was that she was jaded and weary—she had the look of a wounded animal that might bolt if anyone moved too quickly.

One sunny morning, I invited her to take a walk around the lake. As we walked, we shared back and forth the stories from our life, each story led to the next and opened her up bit by bit. As she told me about her family whom she'd been moved away from, she said almost in a whisper, "I don't matter to anyone."

Her words pierced right through my heart. How tragic that she would feel so worthless. I puzzled in my mind how to demonstrate her value to me, to her family, and mostly to God, regardless of what she believed about herself. Out of my pocket, I pulled a twenty-dollar bill and held it out to her. "What do you think this is worth?"

"Duh!" She dropped her jaw in true teen fashion. "Twenty dollars."

"You are correct," I said and crumpled the bill in my hand. Then I threw it down in the dry, Texas dirt and scuffed it around on the ground with my shoe. I then picked up the cash and dangled it in front of her and asked again, "Now tell me, what is the worth of this bill in my hand?"

Her apprehension showed as she drew her eyes into slits. "Twenty dollars?"

"Exactly!" The value had not changed—it was still worth twenty dollars regardless of the smudges and blemishes. Its value was not in how it appeared or was handled, but by the value the U.S. Treasury had given it. How was her life any different? Her value was not in how she appeared or what had happened to her, but in the value God placed on her. Even though life had scuffed and tattered her self-image, she remained a treasure to God and that would never change.

The young woman believed her life held little value. For too long she had listened to the murmurs and undertones of the world whispering her failures. These voices had taken root and grown like noxious weeds, filling her mind with disparaging thoughts. We, like this young woman, struggle with our self-worth. We too frequently listen to the chorus-of-chaos as the world is all too eager and ready to tell us about our shortcomings.

First John 3:1 tells us, "How great is the love the Father has lavished on us, that we should be called children of God! And that is what we are!" According to the dictionary, the word *lavish* means "to give in large amounts or to bestow profusely." It speaks to the abundance of love that God pours out on our heads. What a delightful reminder! Even when we believe ourselves to be unlovable, as we learn to accept his generous gift of love, it helps calm those rowdy voices in our head.

God has created us distinct and unique. He longs for us to be *okay* with who we are and never lose sight of how he sees us. It's amazing that the Creator of the vast universe cares about us and loves us! His love for us is not unlike a mother's fierce love for her child, and even when that child does something foolish (and whose child doesn't), the mother's love remains. Of course, her strong desire is for the child to grow, learn, and do better, but her love doesn't change. The same is true for God's love; it never changes but remains constant.

Years ago, a poem profoundly touched my life, as I grappled through the initial stages of understanding God's love for me and the value he places on my life. The poem compares the exquisite sound of a violin, when played by a master musician, to the redeemed life of a sinner who is touched by God, the master creator. I recently heard this poem quoted at a church service and was once more reminded of the value of my own life, simply because God has placed his hand in mine. This is the scene as the poem opens:

> Anticipation wanes at the auction house as the auctioneer tentatively holds up an old, beat-up violin and asks for the bidding to begin. He doesn't believe the violin will be worth much money, and as expected, the starting bids are just piddles for the timeworn instrument, only a few dollars, and it gains little steam. After a few minutes, an old gentleman shuffles slowly to the front and asks to take a closer look at the piece. His brows furl and his eyes squint as he examines it; he

makes a few adjustments, tucks it under his whiskered chin and lifts the bow to the strings. The melody he plays is so tender and sweet, it brings tears to the eyes of the listeners; the sound so exquisite it seems almost *otherworldly*. The old man nods as he returns the violin back to the auctioneer, and the bidding begins once more in earnest. The prices being offered now are in the thousands!

The audience is bewildered! The auctioneer, when questioned by them about the change of its value, replies with a soft, knowing smile, "It's simple," he says. "It's the touch of the master."

The poem finishes with a powerful message:
And many a man with life out of tune,
battered and bruised . . .
Is auctioned cheap to a thoughtless crowd,
much like that old violin . . .
He's going once; he's going twice,
he's going and almost gone.
But the Master comes, and the foolish crowd
never can quite understand,
The worth of a soul and the change that is wrought,
By the touch of the Master's hand.
The Old Violin —Myra Brooks Welch, 1921

If only we grasped our own value due to *God's presence* in our life. If only we saw ourselves as he sees us and accepted his gifts of love and compassion, then perhaps we'd view *ourselves* differently. His light shines into the most remote corners of our heart and exposes the lies we too easily believe, the lies that cause us to suppose we are unlovable. Listen instead to *his* voice as he whispers love and faithfulness to us. If God had a gym locker, *our* picture would be taped up inside the door, if he had a smartphone, *our* picture would be his wallpaper! He never stops seeking us, he never stops caring—and oh how he longs to be in a close relationship with us!

He is crazy about each of us!

Three Little Decisions

1.

2.

3.

For Deeper Reflection

What circumstances have caused you to doubt your self-worth? List out several ways God has lavished love in your life?

Reflect on the message of *The Old Violin*; let it remind you of the ways the Master *has* touched your life. Any whisper that tells you otherwise is wrong! Make decisions to quiet those destructive and negative voices in your head.

CHAPTER 23

Self-Absorbed

People that know they are important
think about others.
People that think they are important
think about themselves.

—Hans F. Hansen

Exposed!

Have you ever known someone who would walk up to a circle of women engaged in an intense conversation and jump in and take over? You know the type; the one who assumes she knows what's already been said in the conversation (even though she wasn't a part of it), blurts out her opinion—relevant or not—and commandeers the discussion. Poor manners, you think, not to mention irksome, rude, and obnoxious. And then comes the sting of truth as you realize—you are that someone!

Years ago, when I was a college student, my friend Melanie, a woman I knew well and respected, approached me and said, "Janet, I need to tell you about something that happened after church this morning. You probably didn't realize it, but Anne and I were having a private discussion when you charged in and took over the conversation." As we discussed my actions, she showed me a Bible verse in Philippians 2:4 that says, "Each of you should look not only to your own interests, but also to the interests of others," and gently helped me understand the concept of looking to the needs of others more than my own. I understood from her that, when we are too self-absorbed, it's easy to miss those needs.

Imagine the awkwardness in this moment of "truth." My skin was on fire as I blushed from head to toe, I stumbled through an apology for my insensitivity and thanked her—knowing she was right on the mark. With little regard for anyone else, I had waltzed into their conversation and began talking about my issues and my opinions. Anyone listening closely right here might hear Toby Keith's country hit playing in the background—"I Wanna Talk about Me!" And like the woman in the song who gave little thought to anyone besides herself, the music was playing for me!

Tough lesson you say? Oh yes, it was! Even though I was young and plenty immature, it was time to grow up a little and not be so self-absorbed. Melanie was gentle; she used Scripture to reinforce a godly quality I needed in my life. She taught me a much-needed lesson, whether I liked to hear it or not. It is in these moments we make important choices: will we get huffy and storm away at the *nerve* of someone to say such a thing or will we embrace gratitude for a wise friend who cares and gently nudges us to a better place. Let's face it, self-centeredness kills relationships! When we don't listen well or don't truly care what is happening in someone's life, it keeps us from the give-and-take needed to build a healthy connection.

Think of those people who seem so full of themselves and turn every conversation to their own troubles, which are bigger and "badder" than all others. At times, it's difficult to connect with them on a deeper level. But before we start listing all the people we know who are lacking social awareness, let's consider what my dad always said, "When we point our finger at someone, three more fingers are pointing right back at us!" It's better to first take a good look at our own tendency toward self-absorption in our conversations and then determine what steps we can take to grow.

The poignant quote by Maya Angelou, helps us rethink our interactions with others. "I've learned that people will forget what you said, people will forget what you did, but people will never forget how you made them feel." When we take little notice of the people around us, why would we then expect them to take interest in us? When we want to tell them about an award we've won, how cute our grandchildren are, or about a great deal we got on a pair of shoes, if they haven't sensed *our* interest and concern—why would we expect concern or interest to come back from them?

Consider the concept of the *Love Bank* discussed in the book, *Love Busters*. When we do the right thing, or say something positive in a relationship, it's as if we make a *deposit* into their love bank, which then allows a *withdrawal* in the event we do or say something negative. If we have made inadequate deposits, then there's not much there to cover us when we need it. As we watch for the needs of others and strive to meet those needs, it's like making a deposit in the relationship bank—it will come back around to bless us in those times we need reassurance or a shoulder to lean on.

In his book *The Pursuit of Attention*, sociologist Charles Derber addresses the difference between a *shift-response to a shift-support* in conversation. People who are overly self-centered will easily fall into the former rather than the latter. It goes something like this:

> One morning at a local coffee house, Stacy confides in her friend, "I'm so upset with Ruth!"

With the speed of a comet, her friend Cindy responds, "I've never liked Ruth, she's so annoying! I've unfriended her on Facebook." (shift-response)

Cindy has shifted the response right around to herself with little concern about what is going on with Stacy or why she's upset with Ruth. Shift-response is Cindy's attempt to turn the conversation onto what *she* wants to discuss, that being her dislike of Ruth and why she finds her annoying. It's like the example at the beginning of this chapter (but let's not bring it up now and turn it back to the topic of me . . . see how easily this happens?).

Check out the other option:

Stacy shares, "I'm so upset at Ruth!"

Cindy responds in a voice resonating compassion, "Oh no! I'm so sorry to hear that, Ruth has been your friend for years! Is there anything you'd like me to pray about? Please know it will stay between God and me." (shift-support)

Now Cindy listens and shows support for Stacy who is expressing a difficulty with Ruth. This response (shift-support) keeps the focus of the conversation on the one who is sharing in a supportive manner.

Which best describes our day-to-day conversations: *shift-response* or *shift-support*? Becoming more attentive toward others takes practice and thoughtfulness, but keep in mind, the effort we expend is well worth it, as we enjoy a certain depth and connection in our relationships.

Listed below are some ideas that may help us become more supportive and *others*-focused:

- Listen to what the person is really saying.
Practice empathy. "Walk a mile in their shoes," as the old saying goes. When someone shares about an issue going on in her life, stop and think what she might need in that moment. Listen closely, contribute and ask clarifying questions that pertain to her situation. Try to stay on topic and stay fully present in the moment.

  A speaker once claimed our attention span is about seventeen seconds long! If this is true, it will take determination on our part to stay connected with what the other person is saying. A group of physicians now say young people who constantly text, tweet, and use Instagram have the attention span of nine seconds—one second longer than a goldfish.

- Pay attention to people's reactions and body language.
If we dominate a conversation, people will probably back away from us, or find ways to cut the conversation short. We might sense a tone in their voice that seems off or their arms will cross or there will be a crease between their eyebrows. I once spoke with a fellow whose wife had traveled out of state to care for an ailing parent. When asked how his wife was holding up under the strain of a sick parent, he began a litany of frustrations about how hard it was for him to function with her gone. After a couple more attempts to inquire about his *wife's* situation, he turned it right back onto himself, and I slowly backed away.

- Display modesty about your accomplishments.
When we achieve something big or exciting, we might feel a tendency to brag, but it's wise to proceed with a good degree of caution. Bragging does have the innate ability to come across as haughty, even if it's not our intention. We might instead try to communicate a sense of feeling

honored about the accomplishment. More than likely the achievement wasn't done in a vacuum, so find ways to give God and others some credit for the help and support they gave. This shows gratitude for the accomplishment and helps us not seem boastful. On the other hand, we don't want be *fake* in our modesty or it will sound as if we're fishing for a compliment.

- Become a thoughtful person.
  Show genuine interest in others—simple actions speak loudly. Take time to consider what may help another person feel encouraged and supported. It could be simply listening to their story or bringing them a flower. We might send a postcard while on vacation or write an encouraging Post-it note and stick it on a coworker's desk. Be the one who brings bagels to work, remembers birthdays, or helps pack boxes for a friend who is in the exhausting process of a move. I know of a woman who brought a small plant to a friend who had just gone through a rough breakup with her boyfriend. It didn't change the circumstance; it didn't stop the pain. But it simply showed she cared and that was enough at the time.

In general, follow the adage, "Be somebody who makes everybody feel like somebody." Take heart, this is a learnable trait! The reward is great when we have close friends who return our care and genuine interest. Each of us, with practice and intention are able to enjoy such friendships.

Be the person who builds meaningful relationships.

Three Little Decisions

1.

2.

3.

For Deeper Reflection

Do you know someone whose conversation is most always self-centered? Have you ever been that someone? Has anyone ever tried to help you overcome the tendency to be self-centered? How did you respond to their attempt?

How can you pay attention to the shift-support verses shift-response in conversation?

What are specific ways you might show genuine interest in those around you?

CHAPTER 24

Mistakes Happen

*The greatest mistake you can make in life is
to continually fear you will make one.*

—Elbert Hubbard

Spilled Milk

*Who hasn't experienced knocking over a glass of milk at the dinner
table? Everyone seated jumps out of their chair, then rushes forward
to mop up the mess that runs around every plate and onto the floor.
One night at dinner, this happened to one of our young daughters.
As soon as the glass of milk tipped over her big blue eyes widened
with the, "Uh-oh, I'm in trouble" look.*

*Tom noted her dread, shrugged his shoulders, and calmly
said, "Sometimes, mistakes happen!" He then tipped over his own
glass, spilling its contents across the table, then down to the floor
onto his shoes.*

*Now all our eyes widened! The other kids couldn't believe
Dad had tipped his glass over on purpose! All at once, the rest of
us tipped ours, while we laughed and gasped for air. At this point, I
noticed a wide river of milk spilling over the side of the table like a*

waterfall and splattering onto the floor. I jumped up and grabbed the nearest towel as the laughter echoed across the kitchen.

After we all worked to clean up the huge mess, we had a lively conversation about "when mistakes happen." Each of us gained some needed perspective about ways to learn from our mistakes (and the mistakes of others) and how God's views us and loves us despite our mistakes. Lastly we discussed ways to overcome mistakes and not beat ourselves over the head because of them. Our grown kids remember that night at the kitchen table with a sense of fondness, a life lesson not quickly forgotten. At times, they tease their dad about it, but none of them is surprised he did such a thing. For years he has taught and modeled God's unconditional love.

It may start when we are young with just a glass of spilled milk, but when we make a mistake as an adult, it may be difficult for us to own it. We may pretend it didn't happen or we raise our defensive shield and blame others or make absurd excuses for our missteps. We might also attempt to cover up any perceived flaw or weakness and hope no one will notice. Any of these responses have the potential to hurt us in the long run. If we won't *own* our mistakes, it gradually weakens our entire moral fiber and whittles away our strength of conviction.*

To overcome excuse making, understand there is a subtle difference between a reason and an excuse. An excuse quickly shifts the responsibility away from oneself, blaming others or defending our position. A reason given, states facts and an explanation infused with a willingness to take responsibility.

Consider this example: The boss calls an employee into the office and states the employee has poorly handled a sensitive customer service issue. This employee can respond with excuses and blame or with reason and responsibility. It might look like this:

- Make excuses, blame others, and deflect any bad behavior: "When I was trained for this job, no one ever told me how to handle such a snarky customer."
- Share the reason for the error and take responsibility for the behavior. "I was not prepared for the customer to be so angry. I realize I didn't handle it well and lost my temper."

Excuses fly like a kite without a string, and we are unable to get a grip on what really occurred (which may be exactly what the excuse maker wants). In the moment, it seems easier to make excuses rather than take responsibility for what we've done. But know this, all our excuses will, like the kite, eventually crash to the ground. The truth will be exposed, and the mess to clean up becomes much bigger than the original mistake.

How refreshing it is to interact with a person who takes responsibility or with someone who willingly owns their mistakes even though it is easier to blame others or the circumstances. For example, when we drive faster than the speed limit, do we imagine what excuse we'll give to the officer if by chance we are pulled over? Not one excuse works. "Um, sorry officer, running late! . . . The music was so loud! . . . I was just rocking out with Tina Turner. . . . I didn't notice the speed limit sign. . . . The speedometer is broken." No—none of these will work. We are still breaking the law, and the ticket is a means to (hopefully) change our tendency to speed.

A few thoughts about owning our mistakes:

- Accept that mistakes occur in *every* life. We need not fear conceding our own.
- Admit the mistake to whoever needs to know. Don't attempt to cover it up, defend it, or make excuses. Own it.

- Think about what might be learned from the mistake. Embrace this newfound wisdom, and grow from the experience.
- Practice patience about the mistake. If appropriate, learn to laugh about it. Realize, berating or belittling ourselves will not change the mistake.
- Believe God helps us work through any consequences of a mistake. Ask him for wisdom to accept those consequences and for the sense to not repeat it. Remember how powerful he is, and trust that his plan will work as we make reparations.

Imagine what it would be like if we admitted and took ownership for our blunders and stopped the excuses. Picture the incredible growth we would experience as a result! Taking responsibility for our actions will always be valued by those around us and will give us a leg up in personal growth and maturity.

How refreshing to interact with those who take responsibility for their actions.

Three Little Decisions

1.

2.

3.

For Deeper Reflection

Think about the blunders you've made and hate to admit. Which excuses have you made? How could you take more responsibility for them? Can you think of a mistake you made in the past and can now laugh about?

Have you made a mistake and had someone treat you with graciousness despite the mistake? How can you be more gracious with others?

*Note: If you experience extreme fear of making mistakes due to some earlier trauma or severe mistreatment, it may be helpful to seek professional counsel.

CHAPTER 25

Compromised Convictions

Appear as you are. Be as you appear.

—Eastern Proverb

Moral Backbone

A businessman had a successful construction company, but he was often deceitful about deals and deadlines to win the lucrative job bids. Years into his career, the man endured a near-death experience, which opened his eyes to his mortality, which in turn led to a powerful conversion to Christianity. As he made these life-changing decisions, it became clear to him that certain business dealings needed to drastically change. He realized deception was no longer acceptable and vowed to become an honest Christian businessman, regardless of the financial consequences.

Uncertain how it would affect his company, he surged forward with this newfound conviction. To his surprise, an unexpected benefit arose—he felt calm and peaceful deep inside. When asked about it by a fellow believer, the businessman stated, "Now, I always tell my customers what is true, about the price, supplies, or time constraints. It seems like such a little thing, but it amazes me how much less stress I feel since I don't have to try to remember what lies I told anyone or worry about being trapped in an untruth. Since I now always tell them what's true, it's always true." What a healthy approach this businessman discovered: always honest equals always honest.

This man learned a valuable lesson about the peace available to us when we make the right choice. More than likely, this businessman did not start his career choosing to be deceitful with his customers. It probably started with a small lie, which led to another and then another. The little lies and small concessions always seem harmless at first, but they lead to more and more compromise. Eventually, we look in the mirror and do not see the person we set out to be.

Few would readily admit they are dishonest; yet, the prevalence of dishonesty pops up everywhere along with an underlying acceptance and allowance of such behavior. A speaker once asked his audience to raise their hand if they believed honesty was a *top five* conviction they personally held and expected from others. Every hand in the room went up. Then the speaker asked how many of them were honest 100 percent of the time? (There was nervous laughter as he reminded them to be completely honest.) Zero hands went up to this question. 90 percent? No hands still. 80 percent? A few hands began to rise as the percentage dropped. Why do we *claim* to be honest, say it's essential, demand it from others, and yet allow ourselves to compromise?

Similarly, think of the story of the mother who told her three-year-old, as he reached into the candy dish, "Do not eat any candy until after supper."

"Okay, Mama. I just want to hold it for a while."

Minutes later the mother noticed the young boy had unwrapped the candy. "Son, you may not eat the candy until after dinner."

"Okay Mama, I just wanted to smell it."

Not much more time went by when the mother watched him pop the candy in his mouth. Sternly, she said, "I told you not to eat the candy until after dinner."

As she removed it from his little mouth, he looked up, his eyes wide, "But Mama, I just want to hold it in my mouth!"

Maybe this seems like a trivial example, but the idea is this— we get off course when we allow ourselves to give in to the *little* things, and though they seem insignificant they easily become bigger and may turn into harmful habits, if we aren't watchful. A little lie, a little flirt, a little theft is all it takes to start us down a path to where the strong convictions we hold right now become easily compromised. Much like whittling a stick that creates a reedy, breakable twig, just one thin shaving at a time, if we continue to whittle away at our ethical mores, we may find ourselves with a brittle *spiritual* backbone, which snaps under pressure.

Those who won't compromise, but instead choose honesty and integrity are at times mocked and assumed to be weak— yet the opposite is true. It takes courage to be honest, to admit wrongs, and to speak the truth. It's easy to choose a weaker path and go with the flow. But where does that bring us? Years ago, new to the job, my boss asked me to tell a caller he was not in the office. But since he *was* in the office, I respectfully told him I wouldn't say what was not true. This made him angry, but I held my ground and said we'd need to find something else to tell the caller. At that point, he said it was time for lunch, walked out the office and yelled through the closed door, "I am not in the office!" I picked up the phone and honestly told the caller he was at lunch and took a message. Of course, the boss wasn't too happy that day, but a respect grew between us as he now had confidence that whatever I told him would be true.

What if we refused to fall prey to dishonesty and weak convictions? Imagine what might be accomplished in our life!

Developing steely convictions won't happen because we *hope* for it or by simply *wishing* we were stronger. To be a woman with strong convictions means every day we make small decisions to do what is right, even when it's *easy* to settle for the easier way. If we want to have a sturdy spiritual backbone, compromise is not negotiable.

Another story comes to mind of the preschooler who was put down for a nap. One hour later the mother came into the room only to find one of the storybooks torn to shreds behind the child's bed.

> The mother asked, "Who tore this book?"
>
> The child, hearing the serious tone in his mother's voice, replied with shrugged shoulders, "I don't know."
>
> After more back and forth about this, the mom was unsure how to convince her child to be truthful. She asked again, "Tell me, what did God see?"
>
> This was all the child needed as the sobbing began along with the confession, "God saw me tear the book!"

We learn a simple lesson from this young child; anytime we struggle to be honest, we can ask ourselves, *What does God see?* Hebrews 4:12–13 reminds us that God knows the *thoughts and attitudes of our heart* and *nothing is hidden from his sight.* Sometimes we can fool the people around us, but we can never fool God. And since our aim is to please him, we can take our cue from knowing he knows the truth! We can choose to be honest and full of integrity, even though at times it feels difficult.

The more we do what is right, the more our *spiritual backbone* is strengthened and the probability of moving in a more desirable direction will increase. Pick an area we want to improve upon and take a step. Remember, if someone isn't honest in the little things, more likely than not, they won't be honest in the big things.

Big step or small, it doesn't matter; forward progress is forward progress

Three Little Decisions

1.

2.

3.

For Deeper Reflection

How important is honesty to you? In which areas do you struggle to be honest, with yourself? With others?

In what ways might you be whittling away at your ethical backbone? What can you do to become a woman with a strong moral backbone?

CHAPTER 26

Dunderhead Moments

No one can make you feel inferior without your consent.

—Eleanor Roosevelt

Don O'Treply

One year while searching for a job, I asked my friend Lisa about openings where she worked. She mentioned a couple possibilities with her company, so I went online and applied. The next day I received an email reply from Don O'Treply, who thanked me for applying with them and said they would be in touch to discuss my resume. Encouraged to get such a quick response, I called Lisa to tell her about the email from Don, and wondered if she might put in a good word with him. She replied there was no one named Don at her company and she didn't know what the email was about. Well, that seemed odd, but energized by the email and unfazed by her response, I continued to apply at numerous online job sites.

I found it peculiar; when from two different companies I also received email responses from this Don fellow. It led me to look more closely at the email address. Imagine my embarrassment when I reread it a few more times, "donotreply." DoN o tReply. Do Not Reply. Do not reply? No! Not Don O'Treply at all, but Do Not

Reply! Holy Smokes! It was just a standard email to which I should not reply!

My face flushed as red as a hothouse tomato! Even though it was an innocent mistake, all thoughts quickly turned negative—who would want such a dunderhead to work for them? It wasn't a big error, but was enough for me to feel incredibly stupid and insecure. I dreaded telling my friend, worried what she might think about me or tell others.

How easy it is to get down on ourselves when we have those *dunderhead* moments—but know this, everyone has them! But truthfully, just knowing everyone else makes mistakes doesn't stop the drumbeat of negativity pounding in our head. What too frequently happens when we mess up is we fall into a cycle something like this:

- We make a mistake.
- We beat ourselves up with negative self-talk.
- We worry about what others think due to the mistake.
- We berate ourselves some more.

Worry and self-repugnance will never change who we are or what we've done; it only holds us in a tiresome cycle of feeling awful about ourselves. It's like we've painted ourselves into a corner of a dark room, and we can't get out. Instead of giving into the gloom of our blunder, what if we took a cue from Philippians 4:7 and allowed God's peace to take the place of our worries? Here is what the verse says: "The peace of God, which transcends [surpasses] all understanding, will guard your hearts and your minds in Christ Jesus." It is incredible that God's peace can guard our hearts (emotions) and minds (thoughts). To attain this peace, we take on a different mindset, as stated in the preceding verse, "Do not be anxious about anything, but in everything, by prayer, . . . with thanksgiving, present your requests to God." This is how we alter the exasperating cycle of insecurity and then better approach the pesky patterns of *negative self-talk* and *overconcern about what others think.*

Negative Self-Talk

When we allow negative self-talk to reign in our head, the habit, though easily practiced, is tough to break. It reminds me of the time I was driving home from an appointment. My mind was distracted as I thought about all that needed to be done once I got there and the turn I needed to make came up sooner than expected. I quickly braked and maneuvered around the corner, hearing a horn blare. The man in the car behind me veered past and angrily shook his fist. Embarrassment hit and I cringed when I considered what he must have thought about the crazy woman driver in the rusty, green Subaru. Ugly thoughts about myself flew across my mind—how stupid, how inattentive, what a bad driver I am. But never once did the thought occur to me that maybe he was driving too close behind me, texting, or perhaps in need of some anger management! No doubt, he only thought about me for a nanosecond. But here's the thing to ask, am I stupid, inattentive, or a bad driver? No, not any of those—it was just a mistake. But how easily the ugly words burst forth and found me muttering dreadful things.

In a health and nutrition course, one woman shared how her struggles with her weight wrecked her self-esteem. She said it wasn't uncommon for her to feel angry about her image and call herself a fat pig. Several of us in the room were surprised at her brave admission, but then agreed how it was easy for all of us to say ugly things like this. The wise instructor took a few minutes to discuss these tendencies and asked us to consider why we make such unhelpful and self-depreciating comments? She asked us if we would ever say such ugly words to someone we loved? Would we say this to our child, a cherished grandparent or a lifelong friend? Everyone vehemently answered no! "Why then," she continued, "do we say such horrid things to ourselves?" It's a valid question, one we should carefully contemplate.

The good news is we can adjust our thought patterns as well as our word choices. It's a learnable skill, and when we practice being gracious and kinder, we'll see positive results. Then when we hear that inner voice say some ugly remark, we are able to more quickly turn it around. For example, if an exercise class is missed, we don't derisively think, *How lazy can one person be! This is not the way to get in better shape!* Instead, we turn it right on its head and think, *Don't give up, keep at it. Every little bit makes a difference!* Even if positive thoughts seem foreign right now, keep working at finding something constructive, and the habit will stick.

Overconcern about What Others Think

Who really knows the thoughts of anyone else? Even if we did know, we could never control those thoughts, so why try? What about *our* opinions and what *we* think? That matters too! A popular quote resonates loudly in this arena, "What other people think of you is none of your business." Profound and true, yet how many times do we let their estimations affect us? It is amazing how quickly our *perception* of what others think fills us with self-doubt and insecurity. Such overconcern with others' opinions adds unneeded stress to our lives. Why do we give their opinion such a wide berth in our head?*

Mother Teresa posted the following poem on the wall at the orphanage in Calcutta, India, where she faithfully served the poor. It's a reminder to make right decisions no matter what others may think.

Do It Anyway

People are often unreasonable, illogical, and self-centered;
forgive them anyway.
If you are kind, people may accuse you of selfish, ulterior
    motives;
be kind anyway.
If you are successful, you will win some false friends and
    some true enemies;
succeed anyway.
If you are honest and frank, people may cheat you;
be honest and frank anyway.
What you spend years building, someone could destroy
    overnight;
build anyway.
If you find serenity and happiness, they may be jealous;
be happy anyway.
The good you do today, people will often forget tomorrow;
do good anyway.
Give the world the best you have, and it may never be enough;
give the world the best you've got anyway.
You see, in the final analysis, it is between you and your God;
it was never between you and them anyway.

The last phrase is powerful—it is and always has been between us and God. What God thinks and believes about us is what matters, regardless of any blunders we make. As we learn to embrace his plan, his peace will flow more freely in our mind. Here's the bottom line, it takes time and persistence to gain the skill of worrying *less* about what others think. It takes determination to not let the opinions of others impact our thoughts and emotions in negative ways. It also helps when we accept we are all PIPs —People-in-Progress. As the dictionary puts it, progress is the process of improving or developing something *over time.*

Remember—everyone is a PIP.

Three Little Decisions

1.

2.

3.

For Deeper Reflection

When you make a mistake, what kind of negative self-talk stomps around in your head?

In what ways are you overconcerned with other people's opinions?

With focus and attention, you are able to turn negative self-thoughts into positive ones. It may take some time to learn this new habit, but remember, you are a PIP.

*I'd like point this out: each of us knows people who *don't* dwell on things they've done wrong, don't worry about what others think, and wonder what all the fuss is about. Are these people in denial of their faults or do they simply have a healthier perspective on life?

My husband, Tom, is one of these people. Like water off a duck's back, most frustrations, hurts, and disappointments roll off him with nary a second thought. For years, I thought he was tucking it all away and it would erupt one day like Mount Vesuvius. I was wrong. He simply is not affected by such drama. Sure, he feels disappointment and hurt, but he's not a *wallower* like me. He can shrug his shoulders and say, "It is what it is," and on he goes. This mindset baffles me. I find it hard to grasp the uncomplicatedness of such thoughts, but I'm grateful to learn from him and take a page from his book as I overcome my own insecurities.

CHAPTER 27

Be True to You

Today you are you, that is truer than true.
There is no one alive who is you-er than you.

—Dr. Seuss

Truth in the Parking Lot

As a student at the University of Colorado, I connected with a Bible study group on campus. We became a close-knit bunch and worked hard to help each other make better life choices. At some point, I became aware of a tendency to tell "untruths" about myself, which I thought made me appear stronger to those in our group. (My half-baked logic: if they don't know my weakness, maybe they'll think I am stronger.) As these untruths continued unchecked, they became a habit of stretching the truth, giving false impressions, and telling outright lies. I knew being deceptive was not what God wanted me to be. So to break out of this ugly pattern, I decided whenever I said anything untrue, I'd quickly remedy it by saying what was true. In doing this, the truth would be brought into the light and my bad habit reined in.

It wasn't long until an opportunity presented itself. One Sunday after church ended, I said goodbye to this cute guy and told him I had prayed for him every day. He seemed sincerely grateful, gave me a hug goodbye and I was on my way. As I neared my car, the truth hit—there had been no prayer for that guy, I'd just wanted him to think well of me, wanted to appear more "spiritual." The earlier decision to not tell untruths buzzed around in my head as the car keys jingled between my fingers—should I stick to my guns and be honest or let the cute guy think I was something I wasn't?

After what seemed like several minutes, I tromped back inside, found the guy, and in one long nervous breath, said, "You know, when I said I had prayed for you every day? Well, it wasn't true—that didn't happen, and I'm sorry I said it did—but I will pray for you every day this week."

His response is not clear in my memory, but I know I felt deeply embarrassed about the dishonesty. Even though I'll never know what he thought about the admission, something changed deep inside of me. I was on the road to replacing a bad habit and strengthening my spiritual backbone. (By the way, I did pray for the guy!)

Why would a young girl spend so much energy trying to impress a boy? Some call it immaturity, others call it insecurity. Either way, when we want so badly to be liked and accepted, sometimes we lie and spend our energies attempting to be someone we are not. Looking at this example, what were the possible outcomes of going back inside and being honest with the cute boy? He may have walked away, disgusted, or he may have thought it was silly to have lied in the first place. Another possibility—the guy may have been inspired to take a look at his own level of honesty and let my courage boost him to act more honestly in some part of his own life. Actually, it doesn't really matter what he thought because I was on my way to embracing honesty.

Too many of us accept the flawed logic that says, if we present a false front and someone rejects us, they'll only reject the façade and not our true self. The tragedy of this faulty thinking is this: we all long to be loved and accepted for who we truly are, but since we so keenly fear rejection, we hide and allow people to know only the *made-up* us. We are afraid if we lower our masks and reveal the truth about ourselves—people might reject the real us. We believe this would crush us beyond our ability to cope.

Who doesn't have weakness and shadows lurking in the corners of our minds? We tend to be embarrassed by those skulking stalkers and we worry what others will think if they found out. And at times we feel frustration because we've attempted to change these flaws and failed.

Catch those words: embarrassed—worry—frustration—failed

Each of these are real emotions we experience from time to time, but it's not at all how God wants us to live! He knows everything about us (yes, even those lurking shadows), and yet he still loves us and wants to lift us out of the mar of embarrassment, worry, and frustration! The choice is ours to make: we can face those weak areas head on and allow God to change us from the inside out, or we can attempt to hide our weaknesses and live with the constant fear that our shortcomings might somehow be exposed.

When we drop the false pretenses, we then become truly known—our authentic selves are there for others to know and love. It was Oscar Wilde who wrote, "Be yourself—everyone else is taken." Can we finally relax and allow people to get to know the real us? Many accomplish this when they participate in some sort of small-group setting—a book club, study group, or house church. When we attend only large functions, it's easy to get lost in the bigness and be lonely in our incognito.

Over the years I've enjoyed various small group settings where we regularly met, laughed until we cried, cried until we laughed, and talked about what mattered. Thinking of a group in Rhode Island brings up cherished memories. Five couples met most Monday nights for a time and shared our lives, discussed our struggles, and laughed at the craziness of it all. (At the time, each couple had kids from toddlers to teens—which explains much of the craziness.) We talked about raising kids, our jobs, and the state of our marriages. One night, in order to strengthen our interactions with our spouses, we divided the men and women and each group designed a calendar filled with ways we might better serve our spouses for the next seven days. This may sound idyllic, but it was uproarious as we attempted to develop this calendar not according to what *we* wanted but what we thought our spouses would appreciate. On other nights, we jumped in the hot tub at our friend's house—oh, the deep discussions we would have out under those New England stars, coupled with the laughter and the tears. The treasure was being known and loved and accepted for who we truly were.

In another scenario, there was a young woman, who after moving to a new city, joined a small group being organized through her church. She did this to *belong* but also to *be known*. The first group she joined was too brutal in their *truth telling* for what she needed at the time. Another felt too shallow and was made up of people in a completely different phase of life. It took inner courage to leave the *herd* and go in search of another until she found the one that fit her needs. Though it may take a few attempts, the benefit is worth the time spent to find the right setting, to be involved, and to not isolate oneself. The smaller group lends itself to more personal conversations and the chance to tell our true stories. This is how we become known and give people the opportunity to unconditionally love us. It's a dependable way to build closer friendships.

It takes a brave person to become known and courage to accept ourselves the way we are. It is important to remember this: we've all been brought into this world completely unique. Few aspects of our being can be altered—we are who we are: brown-eyed, short, smart, opinionated, daring, cautious, controlling, timid, fearful, or funny . . . For purposes he best understands, God breathed a distinct breath of personality, capability, and quality into each of us. The sooner we can accept how he's made us, the sooner we will be at peace in our own skin and allow others to know us. A preacher once said, "God doesn't give us gifts and talents for us to simply possess them, but he wants us to find a purpose and a way to use those abilities. Once we let go of the pretending game, we'll be better equipped to meet the needs of others around us."

God is light. He asks us to bring our life into his light, or more simply put, not hide in shadows. In 1 John 1:7 we are exhorted to *walk in the light*. I firmly believe, if we are willing to be honest and bring our true selves into the light, we will enjoy greater inner peace and build lasting relationships with others.

In her book *The Wholehearted Journey*, author Denise Bissonnette writes a brilliant quote about dropping pretenses and masks:

> What if we declared this next year as the year of true faces? Perhaps, just perhaps we would find hundreds of new ways to use our hands in shaping the beauty of the world because we would no longer need them for holding up the masks.

As we push past our embarrassment and fear, as we find ways to drop our masks and let people know who we truly are, it heightens the possibility of deeper connections. It's okay to take little steps. Use caution; pray for courage and wisdom.

When we are honest, it allows others to know and love our authentic self.

Three Little Decisions

1.

2.

3.

For Deeper Reflection

Have you tried to change some part of your life and failed?

Which areas of your life do you attempt to hide and cover up?

Who are you allowing to know the *real* you? Who is someone with whom you are comfortable, someone you might speak with and share some areas of struggle?

What could your hands do if they were freed from holding up a mask?

CHAPTER 28

Closer Inspection

What lies behind you and what lies in front of you,
pales in comparison to what lies inside of you.

—Ralph Waldo Emerson

Out of the Fog

One rainy spring we had several hours of dense fog settle around the neighborhood. We'd had days of hard rain, and it was as if the ground could not absorb one more drop. At this point, the moisture was forced to simply hang in the air and cloister everything with its permeating damp.

Structures across the field behind our house were dull shades of gray; the mist blurred the trees into shadows scarcely visible. Any time you are in fog, you feel anxious and vulnerable in the thick soup; not knowing what might be lurking in the gloom. When you drive in heavy fog you are barely able to see beyond the front of your car; you don't drive too fast in the event someone ahead has stopped, but you also don't stop, so as to not be rammed from behind.

It unsettles us when we are unable to see what lies ahead, like the time my three-year-old ingested the contents of a bottle of chewable baby aspirin. At the emergency room, I felt guilty and panicky as they pumped her stomach, not knowing how she would survive the ordeal. As I stood there, helplessly watching the ER crew at work, it was as if I was in fog—unsure how to find a clear way to safety.

When fog settles around us, it feels disconcerting and heightens our anxiety since our vision is hindered and we lose our bearings. Emotional fog is not unlike its physical counterpart. It gathers and thickens by the minute in times when we face a difficult decision, a painful experience, or a frightful call from the doctor. Our vision blurs—we question the path ahead and strain to see beyond the murkiness that envelops us. One upside about fog is how it compels us to focus on what is close at hand and right in front of us. Maybe it's not always a bad thing; perhaps that up close and personal focus prods us to discover things otherwise overlooked.

There was a man who, with no warning and little explanation, was fired from his job. It landed him in an emotional fog; confounded and uncertain, his future felt unclear. This abrupt change forced him to take some time to consider what it was he *really* wanted to do with his life. After spending a few weeks in the gray mist of self-examination, he pursued a job better suited to his personality, moved to a part of the country he loved, and was paid a lot more money! The time spent appraising his situation led him to better clarity.

The saying "Remember in darkness what you learned in the light" may prove helpful when we find ourselves in an emotional fog. As we slow down, even though we cannot see what lies ahead, it's an opportunity to remember what we do *know* and reflect on deeper issues. It becomes a chance to slow down and determine areas needing change or strengthening. Listed below are a few ideas to consider when moving through life's foggy days:

- In the dimness of fog, recall the qualities of God we *know* are true. Even though he feels out of sight, we can be confident he's still there. He doesn't make mistakes, and his plan is always infused with goodness. Hold tight to this thought.

- A time of fog may wake us up to a closer inspection of our physical health, as we make decisions to be more fit or finally make that appointment with a doctor to ask about a nagging physical symptom.

- If our family is somehow being slighted by our inattention and busyness, could the fog slow us down a little bit and allow us to think about the choices we make with our time?

- A foggy period offers an opportunity to consider our boundaries and a chance to determine how we spend our time and with whom we spend it.

- Enjoy the slower pace as a chance to think about future goals and dreams. Moments in the fog may help us picture in our mind where we want to go and who we want to be. Even though it seems obscured right now, give thought to what steps are needed to move closer to that goal.

Author Helen Keller, who was blind, deaf, and mute, admitted, "I cannot do everything, but I can do something; and because I cannot do everything, I will not refuse to do the something that I can." Each of us can do something. When the murkiness of an emotional fog settles around us, our journey may be slowed, our path changed and our vision obscured. This may be a time to allow loved ones to console and comfort us. It's a time to think and pray and be still, then move forward with the decisions that seem best. Use it to catch up on some reading, feeding our minds with Scripture, poetry, or meaningful quotes and allowing the words to soothe us in periods of uncertainty. Sing or listen to songs that reach our souls; pray aloud. Trust the time in fog to bring growth and clarity.

I once read that *a certain darkness is needed in order to see the stars.* What an uplifting notion to realize we don't have to fear the dark of the fog when it sets in, as something beautiful may become visible. This mirthful quote by Eleanor Roosevelt is a simple reminder we need in tough times: "A woman is like a tea bag. You don't know how strong she is until you put her in hot water." An emotional fog may feel like hot water, but we can smile about it, knowing we are becoming stronger than we imagine.

Practice patience, because like natural fog, emotional fog is present in our life for a time and then unexpectedly, it lifts.

Three Little Decisions

1.

2.

3.

For Deeper Reflection

Which qualities of God do you appreciate most? How can you lean into these in times of *fog*?

Think of a time an emotional fog settled into your life. What is a lesson you were able to glean from that time?

What is your reaction to the quote by Helen Keller? What are you still able to do?

CHAPTER 29

Forgiveness for Me

Forgiveness does not change the past,
but it does enlarge the future.

—Paul Boese

Calling from the Past

The phone call came from two time zones away. It was Nita, a young woman who had been a part of a campus ministry we once led. We hadn't spoken in many years and I was happy, if not surprised, to hear her voice. She told me she was enrolled in a leadership training course and one of her assignments was to attempt to "undo" some misconceptions she had about leadership. My happiness at hearing her voice waned as she plunged into the purpose for her call.

Nita told me, "When we were in the same ministry group, you didn't take enough time to understand me and the reasons I was fearful and insecure. It seemed you were often impatient with my struggles." She went on to say she now struggled to lead others, since her skewed recollections of our time together hindered her perception of leadership.

The timing of the phone call was unfortunate, as I was in the middle of packing for another out-of-state move and was distracted by all that needed to be done. But truth be told, I was irked by the call. It frustrated me that she hadn't reached out earlier and now wanted to discuss something from more than a decade before. I offered some apology for my actions and wished her well, wanting to end the conversation as quickly as possible. It put me in a foul mood, which surely came through the phone line loud and clear.

And as often happens when confronted with some prickly situation, I ignored the emotions drummed up by her call and secured them neatly in a box and taped them shut with packing tape. In my head, I disregarded her comments as petty and "not my problem." I didn't genuinely take them to heart nor stop to consider what truths may have been there for me to learn.

It was years (years!) later when I grumbled something to Tom about a woman, Katherine, who had dismissed and disregarded some views I'd shared with her and who was now completely avoiding me. My feelings were hurt due to her unwillingness to sort out our relationship.

As these frustrations poured out of my mouth, Nita's call from years before came bursting forth, unbidden in my mind. The dagger of truth stabbed hard at the memory and brought the scene into sharp focus. My long-ago treatment of Nita was exactly what I was now accusing Katherine of doing to me! The hypocrisy halted my peevish tirade about Katherine and curled my rigid pointing finger back around to me. I was dumbstruck by my insensitivity to Nita. I hadn't accepted her honest thoughts, taken her words to heart, nor listened or cared. And certainly I never appreciated the courage it must have taken for her to make that call all those years ago.

I've been told, life is a series of mistakes and the great thing about a mistake is it offers a fork in the road, a chance to learn and choose one path over another. My eye-opener about Nita now provided a wonderful opportunity to grow, to take responsibility, and to learn from this experience. Unfortunately, that didn't happen. Instead, for the next three days, I circled the drain of self-

contempt; I felt stupid and embarrassed. Around and around went the burbling thoughts, asking how I could call myself a Christian, what kind of friend acts like this, and doubting if this relationship-stuff would ever be figured out? I felt trapped in the pasty muck of self-repugnance!

I had every right to beat on myself, didn't I? Well, no. I'm not some troll sitting under a bridge, uncaring about the damage inflicted on those passing by. But in this situation, I had been self-centered and insensitive to a friend. It was now of paramount importance to remedy the relationship.

I tracked down Nita's number and texted to ask if she had time for a phone call. The conversation, awkward in the first few minutes, led to a glorious conversation, both of us sharing about our life and family. After a while, I mentioned that the purpose of reaching out was my desire to apologize about our long-ago phone call. "I'm so sorry, Nita, for my lack of humility that day and for the reluctance to truly listen as you shared your heart. Will you please forgive me?" I tried to make my words measured and meaningful and not rush through them without taking a breath, as if running for a train.

Out of her kind and loving heart she offered me forgiveness. Oh, the joy that swelled inside! It was as if a thorn deep in my heart was dislodged, I felt lighter and more open.

Once we make a significant step to remedy our blunders, we find the next one a bit tougher—the ability to forgive *ourselves* for that same blunder. We zero in on our list of faults: a poor life decision, an offensive action, a failed relationship, something we didn't do we wish we would have, or something we did do we wish we hadn't . . . the list could go on for days, but what's the point? It's done, it's in the past, we cannot *undo* it. How do we move past such disappointment and forgive ourself, the person who needs it most?

The truth is, we all battle regret about situations we wish we'd handled in a different way. We then struggle to forgive *ourself* and mutter rotten words about our missteps. When I do this, my friend Suzanne gently encourages, "Oh, sweetie, don't say things like that." We need people like this to give us a soft shake, since too often we are unaware our negativity has solidified like clay left out in the noonday sun. It's detrimental to be so unkind with ourselves or remain unwilling to forgive our shortcomings.

It's not that we brush the mistake aside or act like it didn't happen. We simply accept this as a part of life and relationships, we make decisions to let go of disappointment or embarrassment and get to work on the kinder thoughts. Our minds are trainable to this type of acceptance. It's like watching TV. If we don't like the show, we click the remote and *change channels* until we find one we do like. The *choosing* is the key, we hit the search button in our mind and look for those kinder and gentler self-thoughts. And know it's okay (and wise) to call a friend and ask for help when we struggle to find those thoughts on our own. Nothing is gained by holding on to the harmful habit of *not* forgiving ourself. When we find what is good and place our focus on those positive aspects, it grows into a healthier habit. This habit ushers in a peacefulness about ourselves, even when we trip and blunder—notice it's *when* and not *if*.

Plus, what about God's forgiveness? Those of us who follow God's plan believe he forgives us for our wrongs; though this doesn't mean he forgets, he does *choose* to not hold it against us. (This is what mercy means!) What a great relief this is to us. But why are we okay with God forgiving us and then draw the line at forgiving ourselves? Let me clarify, when we forgive ourselves, it doesn't justify our bad choices and certainly there will be consequences. But if God has moved on, isn't it okay for us to do the same?

Sometimes, we simply need to speak the words out loud—words of kindness, mercy, and forgiveness. The spoken word carries great power, and when we hear our own voice say *I forgive myself*, we may be surprised at its powerful effect. Words do matter. Even though it seems awkward, give it a try. Practice saying a prayer like this *out loud*:

> *God, I thank you for your kindness and your forgiveness.*
> *I have made mistakes, and as you forgive me, I forgive myself. I am ready now to stop punishing myself with negative and unkind words. I forgive me. I am ready to practice mercy toward myself.*
> *Thank you for your love and patience in my life.*
> *Amen.*

A preacher once shared about a tombstone he saw in a small county cemetery. The headstone simply said, *FORGIVEN*. No name, no epithet, and no date. But what a statement! Whoever was buried in that place experienced incredible fulfillment and delight to simply be forgiven, so much so, they chose to be remembered for this one fact. Was this *dearly departed* forgiven by an enemy, a spouse, or by God? We will never know about this person, but for us, whether our forgiveness comes from someone we love, from ourself, or from God, it matters not. What we do know is that the joy forgiveness brings into our lives is powerful stuff.

There is a wonderful quote by Charles Spurgeon that speaks to the ways God delivers:

Don't you know that day dawns after night?

Showers displace drought and spring and summer follow winter?

Then have hope! Hope forever, for God will not fail you.

It's amazing to realize we can stop spinning in regret and instead choose tenderness and mercy toward ourselves. In Psalm 32:7, the author writes of his confidence in God, "You are my hiding place; you will protect me from trouble and surround me with songs of deliverance." The change in our outlook becomes brighter, as we release our frustration about our missteps and bask in the thought that God surrounds us and delivers us.

If God has moved on, shouldn't we?

Three Little Decisions

1.

2.

3.

For Deeper Reflection

Has God revealed a blunder you've made? How can you remedy it? About which things are you unwilling to forgive yourself?

Do you believe God has forgiven you for your mistakes or transgressions? In what ways are you able to practice more patience with yourself?

Take a few minutes and practice praying the prayer of forgiveness out loud. How does it free the burden in your heart to say these words?

CHAPTER 30

Unbreakable Lifeline

Hope is faith holding out its hand in the dark.

—George Iles

The Thing with Feathers

In the early years as missionaries in Germany, one of my great worries was about making some huge mistake, due to my language inability. Some wrong instruction or action might cause a setback with the fledgling ministry or cause some great misunderstanding. Anyone who has lived in a foreign country while attempting to learn its language may appreciate some of these challenges and fears.

The small language mistakes were quite embarrassing. Once my husband had a conversation with a gentleman on the subway and subsequently invited him to our home for a Bible study group. In Tom's rudimentary German, he told the man he was a "minister," which the man understood to mean a political "minister"—as in a Finance Minister—and was flattered to be invited to the home of some American diplomat. Imagine his surprise when he showed up and met our Tuesday evening Bible study group!

We also asked people to join us for a Bible study "flu" instead of a Bible study "group" (Grippe not Gruppe), invited them to visit us at the "cherry" rather than the church (Kirsche not Kirche), called our waiter a "plate" (Teller not Kellner), and easily mixed up the words for mustard and cinnamon (Senf and Zimpt). Of course, these were simply embarrassing faux pas.

I worried though, about the consequences of some significant gaffe I'd make, which at times caused me to hesitate to speak up and to second-guess my decisions. As my worries increased, fear coiled around my heart like seaweed wraps around your ankles at the shoreline. At times I was so knotted with fear I didn't want to leave the house. When I spoke with a friend of mine about this paralyzing fear, she wisely counseled, "You've got to remember one thing, Janet. God is bigger than any mistake you could ever make. Whatever missteps, whatever blunders, he is bigger than any of them and is able to help you get over it, around it, or through it!"

I'm sure she said much more, but this truth rang loud in my ears. Oh, it was a needed reminder! Her support and wisdom and objectivity were exactly what I needed to overcome those frenzied fears. She reminded me, God is our secure anchor, our anchor of hope to keep us safe in any storm. For years, her words have remained with me. God is big and always remains near—this is my hope.

Some may suggest hope is only an emotion that waxes and wanes like the light of the moon. But actually, hope in God is far more than a feeling, and though it is a small word, it requires a hefty commitment on our part. Hope means we accept God's genuine care for us, exchanging our fears for hope in his overarching plan. If we are prepared to release the fear and dread clutched tight in our fist, we'll find our hand is freer to hold Gods.

"Hope," according to Emily Dickinson's lovely portrayal, "is the thing with feathers, that perches in the soul and sings the tune without the words, and never stops at all." The dictionary describes hope as wanting something to happen or to be true and to think it *could* happen or be true. It brings a sweet sense of wellness to our soul and helps us breathe a bit easier. The Bible teaches that hope is closely aligned with the word faith. In Hebrews 11:1, the Scripture gracefully knits the two together: "Faith is being sure of what we hope for." What joy we find when we hold on to certainty, knowing God will do what he has promised even when we don't clearly see him working.

The following thoughts may help us hold unbendingly to hope:

- Be determined to believe God is at work even when we cannot *see* the end of the story. It takes personal resolve to hold onto hope and optimism and to trust in his plan.
- Don't give into despair even though our world may seem to be crumbling apart.
- Make a conscious decision, a choice, to embrace hope—it won't alight like a dove on our shoulder without us making effort to discover it.
- Choose to hope again and again, in light of any dismal circumstance. To have hope requires action, it is something we practice, like an athlete who wants to be a champion.
- Remain faithful to God's plan even when we don't understand the *why*. It may or may not crystalize with the clarity of a brilliant gemstone, but whether we gain understanding or not, it is still wise to hold on to faith.

When we stop trusting God's plan and give voice to our doubts, our hope sours, like milk left out in the sun, and we wonder if God will really do what is best for us. This distrust fosters fear and insecurity, and we might question if God is paying attention or even listening to our prayers? We wonder if we matter to him or if he cares about our pitiful situation? Sometimes, amid our fear and doubt, it's difficult to see any good or have hope in anything. In Hebrews 6:18, the *Message Bible* uses the following phrase to describe hope: *an unbreakable spiritual lifeline.* If we can muster even the smallest flicker of hope, it binds us to God and securely connects us to his lifeline.

In a field near my house is a sea of sunflowers. In late summer, the faces of these giant blooms welcome the morning sun and then follow its warmth all day until it sets behind the massive Rocky Mountains. At any time of day, the flowers hold their face to the sun wherever it is in the sky. It's a quiet reminder to keep my eyes on God's plan, to look to him for strength, for ideas, and for support on those problematic days. This is what hope is: we keep our face turned to him and as we do, our confidence grows and courage comes into focus. We understand God is bigger than we are, bigger than our mistakes, and he has a workable plan for our life. We also remember to focus on the eternity of Gods plan which is what makes so many hard days bearable. Of course, it doesn't guarantee all will go well every day, but there's no better alternative than to cling to God's plan nonetheless.

When we hold onto hope, we find an unbreakable spiritual lifeline to God, and like my friend said years ago, "God is bigger than any mistake!" Whatever blunders we make, he is bigger than any of them and is able to get us over it, around it, and through it!

Like sunflowers, we keep our face turned toward God.

Three Little Decisions

1.

2.

3.

For Deeper Reflection

At which times do you struggle the most to believe God is at work in your life?

Do you hesitate to make decisions for fear you might make the wrong one? How does it help to think about God being bigger than any mistake you might make?

What does it mean to you to have an unbreakable spiritual lifeline?

CHAPTER 31

The Corner Piece of the Puzzle

To forgive is to set a prisoner free and discover that the prisoner was you.

—Lewis B. Smedes

Rockslide!

I was at the end of my tether! No matter what I did, no matter how many rewrites, I struggled to complete the chapter on forgiveness. I dismantled the chapter numerous times and put it back together in a different format, to no avail. It seemed I had done the work needed, had spent hours working through forgiveness issues and resolving matters, but still, something niggled at the back of my head and until it resolved, the chapter refused be finished. Finally, in exasperation, I set the whole thing aside to percolate like an old coffee pot on the stove's back burner. In prayer, I asked God to help me figure out where the holdup was and to work in my mind and in my soul to bring about some clarity.

In the meantime, I had asked my longtime friend Kay (who knows me well) to review the introduction to this book to see if I had honestly expressed what Tom and I went through without malice toward anyone. Certainly, there had been times I wanted to include a good bite in the story, wanted others to hear my pain, but since I had forgiven those people and moved on, there was no need for that. The ache about that long-ago, painful experience had been neatly packaged in a box and well secured with packing tape. (And I've had a lot of experience with packing tape!)

Kay responded with some thoughts about one of the paragraphs, and in her sensitive way, said this:

> This paragraph is good, but I think the last sentence is a bit too dramatic and will alienate some readers. It kind of hints at a remaining resentment, and I don't think that's what you're trying to communicate. Just my opinion, of course!

Hmm, remaining resentment? Hadn't this all been dealt with? As I contemplated the sentence in question, I couldn't quite see what she saw, but this was Kay, wise and full of love and kindness. So once more I turned to God, asking him to show me if there was indeed remaining resentment tucked away in a hidden pocket of my heart.

Several days passed and I remained perplexed about the granite wall that stood between me and completing the chapter, unaware how Kay's thoughts whirled in my mind and God's Spirit stirred in my soul. And then, like a pick-axe piercing a capably erected stone wall, a crevice opened, and a thought hit hard: I need to be forgiven!

What? That was weird. Where had that thought come from? Forgiveness? Me? How would that help? The question circled my brain for about seven seconds until the next fissure was exposed. What became crystal clear in that moment was this: years ago, when we were let go from our ministry job, I was, of course, deeply hurt.

But because of that hurt, I justified a lot of anger toward those who did the hurting. At that time (and since), I've prayed and worked to forgive them, because it was the right thing to do. But here is what's true, I still held a grudge and a low-burning resentment about it.

And there it was, that remaining resentment.

Kay's words arose out of the rubble that had fallen from my heart and echoed across my mind. I was thunderstruck and found it hard to breathe! It was baffling, that this remaining resentment in my heart had been so easily tolerated. How could I not have seen this—and been so blind?

It was astounding to see what God had exposed and to experience his incredible patience. Once I caught my breath, I called a friend in tears and half-kidded, half-asked what she thought about this awakening, hoping she might say I was overreacting and to just let it go. She didn't. Instead, she reassuringly said, "Sweetie, you know what you need to do."

Crud, she was right. I did know. I could remain resentful or choose humility, apologize for the lingering resentment, and ask for forgiveness.

Taking steps to resolve a broken relationship is like doing a five-thousand-piece jigsaw puzzle. All the pieces are dumped out, we search and sort to find the edges and then finally a *corner piece.* Something about finding that one piece gives us the confidence our puzzle will indeed be completed, and the picture will come together! As it is with an injured relationship. We seek and discover that corner piece which serves as a boundary line of sorts or a starting place upon which we can build. When we find a little corner piece of an injured relationship, it's as if we find that one thing to say or realize some important lesson and a beautiful reconciliation is realized.

The words of Ephesians 4:2–3 help us know the way to build unity in relationships, and in the realm of overcoming resentment, it knocks our socks off!

> Be completely humble and gentle; be patient, bearing
> with one another in love. Make every effort to keep
> the unity of the Spirit through the bond of peace.

Just the first three words astound us! But this is the call: be
humble (completely!) and gentle, be patient and bear with others.
Could we make this a corner piece in how we move forward in
relationships? Imagine a world where this actually happened,
where we made every effort to keep unity! No more remaining
resentment. No more bitterness or grudges, criticalness or gossip.
Life would be incredible! In 1 Peter 2:23–25, as an eye-witness of
how Jesus lived and died, Peter wrote, "When they hurled their
insults at him, he did not retaliate; when he suffered, he made no
threats. Instead he entrusted himself to him who judges justly."
Wow, another corner piece! No retaliation or resentment here!
Those of us who claim to be followers of Jesus are called to *be like
him*. Since this is the case, we should actually, be like him, even
when we struggle in relationships.

Now that a significant corner piece had been exposed about
my remaining resentment, there were a handful of people who
needed to be called. These were not malicious people, but God-
seeking men and women who had done what they felt was best at
the time. With no small amount of trepidation, I made the calls,
bumbling along, apologizing for my poor reactions so long ago,
but mostly for the remaining resentment. I asked each of them
for forgiveness and incredibly, every one of them expressed a
readiness to forgive and thanked me for the courage to reach out
to them. As each call ended, a deep sigh escaped my chest and I
wondered what had taken me so long!

Why are we often unable to see the misery residing inside
our heart? When we get hurt, our back gets up and we hold so
tightly to the hurt. It's in those times we struggle to see what is
clear and right in front of us, and it's harder yet to respond *well*.

But thankfully, this is where God's wisdom, love, and mercy meet us, in those very moments when we need it most.

The following story offers a powerful message:

The Fable of Two Brothers
(original author unknown)

Once there were two brothers who owned adjoining farms. For years they worked side by side in harmony—sharing equipment, laborers, and various ideas—until one day they had a misunderstanding which grew into an offense and escalated. as angry words were exchanged. After a while, the brothers refused to speak and the rift grew. At one point the younger brother took his bulldozer to the river levee and scraped it out, so the small burbling creek that ran between their properties now filled to a wide river between them, making it impossible to cross.

Weeks later, a carpenter stopped by the older brother's home and asked if he had any woodwork that needed to be done. The brother thought for a few minutes and then replied, "Yes! Take the lumber by the side of the barn and build an eight-foot fence at the edge of the river so I won't even have to look across to my younger brother's property. That will show him how I really feel."

Then the older brother left on a three-day business trip to buy supplies. When he returned, he expected to see a completed wall but to his astonishment, instead of a wall, the carpenter had built a beautiful bridge stretching from one side of the river to the other! The older brother was furious and charged out to confront the old man. Lo and behold, he saw his younger brother walking toward him on the bridge, hand outstretched saying, "Brother! You are quite a man to build this bridge after all the hateful things I've said and done."

The two brothers stood in the middle of the bridge, shaking hands, clapping each other on the back and expressing joy in their reunion, as they saw the carpenter lift his tool box and begin to walk away. "Wait," they said, "we have other projects we'd like you to complete."

The carpenter smiled and said, "I'd love to stay on, but I have many other bridges to build."

When a relationship matters to us, we'll make every effort to find clarity and resolution. At times, we are more like the brothers whose first inclination is to dig rivers and build walls. How grateful we can be for God's perfect plan to show the better solution: a bridge!

It doesn't mean all damage and hurt will simply disappear if we apologize or make a phone call (build a bridge), but it certainly is a good start. Take this into consideration: we are only able to deal with our *own* heart and our *own* reactions. Romans 12:18 says, "As far as it depends on you, live at peace with everyone." We can take needed steps and look for ways to repair what has been damaged. It bears repeating: "As far as it depends on you, live at peace with everyone."

Go build a bridge.

Three Little Decisions

1.

2.

3.

For Deeper Reflection

Are there areas of your life in which you need to make apologies? Why does it take us so long to get to this point in our heart? Pray for God to show you the *corner piece* of the puzzle, to help resolve a broken relationship.

How might you build a bridge where a wall has been?

Looking Back while Moving Forward

The journey of a thousand miles begins with one step.

—Lao Tzu, Chinese philosopher

Moving-Day Prayer

Late in the afternoon when the last items in the house had been packed into boxes and loaded on the truck, Tom and I wandered through the empty house and prayed. We thanked God for the memories shared over the last decade in this home—every room stirred memories of times with the kids and dear friends. Some of the memories were difficult to recall and others reminded us of times of incredible happiness.

In the living room, we thanked God for family gatherings, the Christmas trees, slumber parties—so much mirth shared within those walls, and for the piano that blessed us with hours of music and joy. We wandered to the bedrooms and recalled prom preparations, polka-dot walls and late-night talks. It was in those rooms we crafted Valentine hearts, cried over broken hearts, and learned to love God with all our heart. We gave thanks for the memories of each child and the treasure they are in our family.

Heading to the garden surfaced sweet memories of get-togethers with friends on the patio drinking coffee and sweet tea, groups of teens jumping on the trampoline, jumping into the pool, or making jump shots at the basketball hoop. We prayed with thanks for the garden, the years of bounty it produced, and the fig tree—oh, how I loved that tree, grown from just a twig—and we wept as we bid it farewell.

Our stop in the garage was notable—as we thought about the many hours Tom had tinkered at the workbench, fixed cars and bikes, and helped with school projects. We may have even said a prayer of thanks for the attic—who knows, one day there may be a book about that attic.

Reentering the house, we came to the kitchen and thought of the dailiness of family life—baking cookies, homework at the kitchen table, and dinners when we always shared our highs and lows of the day. Anyone, young or old, who joined us for a meal was asked to join in, much to his or her surprise. We prayed for the countless friends fed from that kitchen and the significant and everyday conversations that occurred around the island, as we chopped, washed, and stirred. Tears streamed down our faces as we thanked God for each one of them. Such sweet memories of sitting around that solid oak table—the stories shared in laughter and tears as so many lives melded there in that place. Our hearts are fuller and our life richer because of those moments.

We finished our circuit on the front porch where we'd said countless hellos and tender goodbyes, where we waved kids off on dates and then later, reluctantly, off to college. Each memory was like a photo, imprinted in our mind filling us with joy. We were astounded to realize how many blessings God had poured out on us—he had not left us alone but had been in each room for every moment and blessed us in this house more than we could fathom.

In rereading the chapters of this book, I was astonished how many of these chapters revealed some hurt I'd endured, some disappointment, and how many times I had fallen headfirst into a pit. At first, it was unsettling to see all the relational issues, and then it was quickly followed by embarrassment, to see so all the drama collected in these pages. I began to wonder if it somehow disqualified me to write a book? But the truth is, in speaking with men and women about their conflicts and difficulties, I don't think all of this is so unusual—each of us struggles to find a way through the dumbfounding challenges thrown at us. This thought encourages me to let go of the embarrassment and follow my own advice!

If I can make small daily decisions to grow, then anyone can!

The *moving-day prayer* is significant, since this home was the one in which I lived when my world shattered, when I feared I may never be whole again. Certainly, there have been many other homes and other prayers upon departure, but this house held certain significance due to the shattering of our life's work, although only temporary. And as often happens, the very thing that breaks us serves as a catalyst to usher in a new mindset.

When our world falls apart, there is nowhere else to turn but to God. These are the times when we are most willing to listen for his voice, ready to surrender, and able to learn the lessons he teaches. We beg God to pull us, drag us, or lift us out of the pit into which we've fallen. The moving-day prayer was a good reminder that I had not been left alone, had learned some needed life lessons, and had grown remarkably, despite the difficulties. I had survived and come out stronger due to the challenge!

This quote has been a favorite of mine for decades:

"Oh God of second chances, here I am again!" (Author unknown)

What a poignant reminder of the fact, no matter how often we fail, no matter how often we blunder or find ourselves on the wrong path, we know and believe with God's help we are *always* able to begin again. And isn't that our goal, after all, to grow and to make progress? God doesn't expect us to have it all figured out *today*, but he does ask us to make good effort to do our best. As we make small, useful decisions, we'll find ourselves moving in the right direction.

Make just *Three Little Decisions* each day and believe with all your heart, God remains by your side for each step! Whether you are ready to act now or simply allow time for deeper reflection, this is your chance to move forward.

Acknowledgments and Thanks

To my mother, Marita Jean. You continue to call me higher and with each passage of my life, you are the one I want to imitate. You have shown me Jesus along the way—I thank God every day he allows our lives to be joined. I love you forever.

For my children, Ben, Lauren, Stephanie, and Jessica, you are wonderful treasures God has gifted to me. Oh, the laughter, the memories, the insights, and the bond we share. Each one of you offers a unique quality, without which my life would be less. I love having you in my life and am inspired by yours.

There was a small group of women who devoted themselves to me in Dallas and helped keep me afloat for months of dark days. They called, they prayed and showed up and gently nudged me back to faith. To Sally O., Margo I., Lane H., and Patty S., only God knows what you did and how long you did it. I couldn't be where I am today without your long-suffering kindness and your tenacious love. "Thank you" hardly comes close to expressing my heart.

To those who read and reread various stages of this book, you are beacons of light on my journey. I trusted you as I bared my soul—you didn't disappoint. Bonny-Marie, Jessica, Kay, Lori, Marty, Renee, Stephanie, and Suzanne, I thank you with everything I hold dear.

I'm thankful for Maggie, who years ago, gave me the checklist of *Three Things to Do Today!* It was the impetus for the seed that grew into this book. I hope you smile down from heaven as you see how God worked through *you* to help me.

To Astrid for giving me the gentle nudge to *write the book already!* Thanks—I needed that.

To those in the many cities and ministries where I had the honor to work. Thank you for your devotion to God and for your service to me. You accepted me and loved me through good times and bad. Many of your stories are in these pages, I'm indebted to you for these life lessons. I remember you: Colorado University, Los Angeles, San Francisco—East Bay, Boston, Providence, Dallas, and Deutschland! You are forever in my heart. Mein Herz ist voller Liebe für Euch.

To my editor and writing coach, Cecile Higgins, I say a huge thank-you! God placed you in my life at just the right time. Your ideas, wisdom, support, and enthusiasm for this project fueled my jets on many occasions. You've helped my dream become a reality.

Bibliography

This bibliography is by no means a complete record of all the works and sources the author has consulted. It indicates the substance and range of reading upon which she formed her ideas, and it is intended to serve as a convenience for those who wish to pursue further study of the topics.

Baker, Don, and Cameron Stauth, *What Happy People Know*. New York: St. Martin's Griffins, 2004.

Bissonnette, Denise, *The Wholehearted Journey: Bringing Qualities of Soul to Everyday Life and Work*. Santa Cruz, CA: Diversity World, 2002.

Chapman, Gary, *The Five Love Languages: The Secret to Love that Lasts*. Chicago, IL: Moody, 2010.

Derber, Charles, *The Pursuit of Attention*. New York: Oxford University Press, 2000.

Dickens, Charles, *A Christmas Carol*. London, England: Chapman & Hall, 1843.

Harley, Willard F., Jr., *Love Busters*. 2nd ed.. Grand Rapids: Fleming H. Revell, 2008.

LaFrance, Marianne, *Why Smile? The Science behind Facial Expressions*. New York: W.W. Norton & Company, 2013.

Luskin, Frederick, *Forgive for Good, A Proven Prescription for Health and Happiness*. New York: Harper Collins, 2003.

Mandela, Nelson, *Long Walk to Freedom*. Boston: Little, Brown, 1995.

Peterson, Eugene H., *The Message Bible*. Colorado Springs, CO: NavPress Publishing Group, 1993–2002

Porter, Eleanor H., Boston: L. C. Page, 1913.

Journals/Newsletters/Articles

Chopra, Deepak. "How to Release the Past and Return to Love." The Chopra Center, accessed April 15, 2016, http://www.chopra.com/articles/how-to-release-the-past-and return-to-love.

Jaffe, Eric. "Why Wait? The Science Behind Procrastination." *The Association for Psychological Science Observer* 26, no. 4 (April 2013), accessed April 23, 2017, www.psychologicalscience.org/observer/why-wait-the-science-behind-procrastination.

Blogs

O'Connor, Anahad, "The Secrets to a Happy Life, from a Harvard Study," Well, *New York Times*, March 23, 2016, well.blogs.nytimes.com/2016/03/23/the-secrets-to-a-happy-life-from-a-harvard-study/

Widrich, Leo, "The Science of Smiling: A Guide to the World's Most Powerful Gesture," Buffer blog, October 2013, blog.bufferapp.com/the-science-of-smiling-a-guide-to-humans-most-powerful-gesture.

68042502R20122

Made in the USA
San Bernardino, CA
30 January 2018